# READING FOR TODAY

*A Sequential Program for Adults*

**Book Six**

## Program Authors

**Linda Ward Beech** • **James W. Beers**
**Jo Ann Dauzat** • **Sam V. Dauzat** • **Tara McCarthy**

## Program Consultants

David C. Bub
Albany-Schoharie-Schenectady B.O.C.E.S.
Albany, New York

Christina H. Miller
Shoals Area Adult Education Program
Muscle Shoals, Alabama

Dannette S. Queen
Office of Adult and Continuing Education
New York, New York

John Ritter
Oregon Women's Correctional Center
Salem, Oregon

Lydia Smith
Adult Literacy Instructors' Training Institute
Los Angeles, California

Betty L. Walker
Richard J. Daley College
Chicago, Illinois

**STECK-VAUGHN**®
C O M P A N Y
A Subsidiary of National Education Corporation

# Acknowledgments

**Staff Credits:**

| | |
|---|---|
| Executive Editor: | Ellen Lehrburger |
| Senior Supervising Editor: | Carolyn Hall |
| Project Editor: | Margie Weaver |
| Design Manager: | Donna Brawley |
| Electronic Production: | Kristian Polo, Shelly Knapp |
| Cover Design: | Pamela Heaney |
| Photo Editor: | Margie Foster |

**Photography Credits:**   p. 8, 24 AP/Wide World; pp. 104, 111, 113 UPI/Bettmann
Phyllis Liedecker
James Minor
David Omer
Rick Williams

**Cover Photography:**   © Stock Market

**Illustration Credits:**   Alan Klemp

**ISBN: 0-8114-9226-5**

# Contents

●  ●  ●  ●  ●

# Contents

# To the Learner

Dear Learner:

You are starting the final book in the *Reading for Today* series. In the *Introductory Book* and *Books 1-5* you learned to divide words into parts and to build new words. This book takes you beyond basic reading skills. In Book 6 you will use the skills you have learned to read articles about interesting people, places, and issues. What topics do you like to read about?

_____

_____

_____

In *Book 6* of *Reading for Today*, you will be reading longer selections and working on exercises designed to strengthen your comprehension skills. You will learn to use the dictionary, a valuable tool in becoming an independent reader. You will also learn to use context clues and your own experience to help you understand what you read. And you will continue thinking, discussing, and writing, all of which are part of reading in today's world.

Your reading skills are getting stronger every day. Think about how reading can help you meet a goal you have set for yourself in daily life or on the job. Now write about it.

_____

_____

_____

# Scope and Sequence

| Book Title | Sight Words/Vocabulary | Phonics/Word Study |
|---|---|---|
| **Introductory Book** | • Visual discrimination of letters/words<br>• Recognition of letters of the alphabet<br>• Sight words in context<br>• Question words (*who, what, when, where, why*)<br>• 157 words total | • Initial and final consonants<br>• Short vowels and CVC word pattern<br>• Long vowels and CVC + *e* word pattern |
| **Book One** | • Introduces 107 sight words, function words, and number words<br>• Reviews 143 words from the *Introductory Book* | • Letter-sound associations reviewed for<br>    Consonants<br>    Short vowels and CVC word pattern<br>    Long vowels and CVC + *e* word pattern |
| **Book Two** | • Sight word pages introduce 63 new words<br>• Review word pages reinforce 143 words from the *Introductory Book* and 107 words from *Book 1* | • Short vowels taught and reviewed through these word families:<br>    Short *a* in *-at, -an, -ad, -and*<br>    Short *e* in *-end, -ent, -et, -ed*<br>    Short *o* in *-op, -ot*<br>    Short *i* in *-in, -it*<br>    Short *u* in *-ut, -un*<br>• Initial consonants reviewed and recycled |
| **Book Three** | • Sight word pages introduce 63 new words<br>• Review word pages reinforce 84 sight words from *Books 1–2* | • Long vowels taught and reviewed through these word families:<br>    Long *a* in *-ake, -ay*<br>    Long *i* in *-ine, -ight*<br>    Long *o* in *-ope, -old*<br>    Long *e* in *-eed, -eat*<br>    Long *u* in *-une, -ute*<br>• Short vowels reviewed through these word families: *-ag, -ell, -ip, -ig, -ug*<br>• Initial consonant blends introduced in context: *st, sh, wh, pr, dr, str, th, cl, tr* |

# of Program Strands

| Language/Writing | Comprehension/Life Skills |
|---|---|
| • Writing letters of the alphabet<br>• Writing words and sentences<br>• Language experience stories<br>• Journal writing | • Finding the main idea<br>• Recalling facts and details |
| • Antonyms<br>• Adding -s to form plurals<br>• Adding -s, -ed, and -ing endings to verbs<br>• Writing sentences<br>• Language experience stories<br>• Journal writing | • Predicting<br>• Summarizing<br>• Recalling facts and details<br>• Finding the main idea |
| • Forming plurals with -s<br>• Adding -s, -ed, and -ing to verbs<br>• Forming contractions<br>• Capitalizing sentences and proper names<br>• Adding 's to form singular possessive of nouns<br>• Doubling the final consonant to add -ed and -ing to verbs<br>• Writing sentences<br>• Journal writing | • **Comprehension skills:** predicting, summarizing, recalling facts and details, finding the main idea, inferring, sequencing events, drawing conclusions, determining cause and effect<br>• **Life skills:** managing money, moving to find work, maintaining health, using leisure time, job safety, understanding self and others, selecting a satisfying job |
| • Compound words<br>• Irregular plurals<br>• Adding -er to nouns<br>• End punctuation of sentences<br>• Irregular verbs<br>• Dropping final e to add -ed and -ing to verbs<br>• Using quotation marks in dialog<br>• Writing sentences<br>• Journal writing | • **Comprehension skills:** predicting, summarizing, recalling facts and details, finding the main idea, inferring, sequencing events, drawing conclusions, determining cause and effect<br>• **Life skills:** finding ways to increase income, rearing children, promoting health care, handling social relationships, learning about training programs, coping with job dissatisfaction, working together for change |

# Scope and Sequence

| Book Title | Sight Words/Vocabulary | Phonics/Word Study |
|---|---|---|
| **Book Four** | • Sight word pages introduce 84 new words<br>• Review word pages reinforce 84 sight words from *Books 2–3*<br>• Life Skill pages introduce 28 new words | • Consonant blends taught:<br>  *r* blends: *br, cr, dr, fr, gr, pr, str, tr*<br>  *s* blends: *sc, sk, sm, sn, sp, st, str, sw*<br>  *l* blends: *bl, cl, fl, gl, pl, sl*<br>• Consonant digraphs taught: *ch, sh, shr, th, wh*<br>• Silent letters taught: *wr, kn, gu, gh*<br>• Long vowels *i* and *e* spelled *-y* taught<br>• Long and short vowels reviewed through these word families: *-ay, -ack, -ank, -ate, -ean, -ear, -eep, -eet, -ight, -in, -ine, -ink, -ing, -ock, -ub, -y*<br>• Syllables defined<br>• Vowel sound as schwa introduced |
| **Book Five** | • Sight word pages introduce 84 new words<br>• Review word pages reinforce 84 sight words from *Books 3–4*<br>• Life Skill pages introduce 30 new words | • Vowel digraphs taught through these word families: *-age, -aid, -ain, -ame, -ape, -ay, -ie, -ice, -ight, -ind, -ive, -ook, -ool, -oon, -ue, -ew, -all, -aw*<br>• Diphthongs taught through these word families: *-oil, -oy, -own, -ound, -oup, -ow*<br>• R-controlled vowels taught through these word families: *-ark, -art, -irl, -ork, -orn, and -urse*<br>• Consonant blends and digraphs reviewed and recycled<br>• Syllables and schwa reviewed |
| **Book Six** | • Definition pages introduce 70 new words<br>• Vocabulary pages cover the following skills:<br>  Multiple meanings    Suffixes<br>  Word stress        Prefixes<br>  Antonyms         Analogies<br>  Dictionary entries<br>• Vocabulary, word study, and life skills pages introduce new words in context | • Dividing words into syllables using VCV, VCCV, and consonant + *le* word patterns<br>• Dictionary entries<br>• Dictionary pronunciations<br>• Dictionary accent marks |

# of Program Strands

| Language/Writing | Comprehension | Life Skills |
|---|---|---|
| • Irregular verbs<br>• Prefixes *re-* and *un-*<br>• Plurals with *-ies*<br>• Suffixes *-ly, -ful, -ness, -y*<br>• Abbreviations and titles<br>• Days of the week and months of the year<br>• Journal writing | • Predicting<br>• Summarizing<br>• Cause and effect<br>• Inference<br>• Stated and implied main idea<br>• Sequence<br>• Context<br>• Drawing conclusions | • Writing a letter<br>• Reading coupons<br>• Reading a report card<br>• Reading a prescription<br>• Reading park rules<br>• Coping with shyness<br>• Reading a schedule |
| • Word building skills reviewed: forming plurals; adding *-s, -ed,* and *-ing*; adding prefixes and suffixes<br>• Adding *-er* and *-est* to adjectives<br>• Writing a friendly letter<br>• Changing *y* to *i* to add *-es, -ed*<br>• Forming plural possessive of nouns<br>• Reflexive pronouns<br>• Plurals with *-es*<br>• Irregular verbs<br>• Journal writing | • Predicting<br>• Summarizing<br>• Fact and opinion<br>• Comparing and contrasting<br>• Sequence<br>• Inference<br>• Making judgments<br>• Drawing conclusions<br>• Classifying | • Reading help wanted ads<br>• Payment schedule<br>• Reading a map<br>• Telephone safety<br>• Reading ads<br>• Filling out a form<br>• Reading a menu |
| • Using adjectives<br>• Writing names and titles<br>• Writing complete sentences<br>• Recognizing fragments<br>• Past tense of verbs<br>• Pronouns<br>• Recognizing run-ons<br>• Journal writing | • Predicting<br>• Summarizing<br>• Recalling facts<br>• Character traits<br>• Main idea<br>• Cause and effect<br>• Inference<br>• Sequence<br>• Drawing conclusions<br>• Writer's tone and purpose<br>• Fact and opinion | • Finding library materials<br>• Registering to vote<br>• Writing a summary of qualifications<br>• Completing a medical form<br>• Filling out a credit application<br>• Being a good listener<br>• Reading abbreviations |

# One Woman, Two Worlds

## DISCUSSION

### Remember

Look at the picture. What do you think a writer such as Sandra Cisneros might share with a reader?

### Predict

Look at the picture and the title. What do you think it means to "live in two worlds"? What do you think the story is about?

**Instructor's Notes:** Read the discussion questions with students. Discuss the story title and the photos.

Sandra Cisneros is a Latina writer and poet. She writes with pride about what it is like to be a Latina in the United States. Other Latinos see themselves in Cisneros's works. Non-Latinos who read her stories learn about Latino culture. But her stories and poems are more than a record of Latinos' lives in the U.S. Cisneros knows two languages and two cultures. This knowledge gives her two different ways of looking at life. These two viewpoints help Cisneros show how two cultures can affect one another. Her poems and stories have the power to make people think in a different way.

## A Writer Grows Up

Cisneros was born in Chicago, Illinois, in 1954. Her father is Mexican. Her mother is Mexican-American. The family often visited her father's mother in Mexico. These visits brought Cisneros closer to her Latino roots. But the U.S. culture still seemed strange to Cisneros. Her teachers didn't understand her first language or her life. As a result, Cisneros didn't do well in school.

**Instructor's Notes:** Have students read the next two pages silently. Have them underline words they don't recognize. Review the underlined words. Explain that the term *Latino* refers to men or to people in general from Latin America and *Latina* is the form of that word that refers to women.

It is a tradition in Latino families for women to live at home until they marry. But when Cisneros grew up, she decided to live by herself. She couldn't think for herself with her father and six brothers watching over her. Her father didn't agree with her decision to live alone. Cisneros wrote a poem about this conflict with her father.

Most of Cisneros's work is about the conflict between the culture of the family and that of the society. People of all races deal with this conflict. They struggle to take on new ideas and ways of life while staying true to their families' beliefs. Cisneros knows the pain this conflict can cause. But she also knows that it is possible to feel at home in both worlds. Cisneros thinks the mixing of cultures can create something new and exciting.

## Moving On

Cisneros lives in San Antonio, Texas. San Antonio is close to the border between the U.S. and Mexico. Cisneros feels at home here because it is a city of two worlds. Latino culture and American culture meet and blend in San Antonio. Like Cisneros, San Antonio has the best of both worlds.

# Vocabulary: Definitions

**Read each paragraph below. Notice how the other words in each sentence help define the new word. Match the vocabulary words with their meanings. Write the letter.**

audience
childhood
commitment
culture
passion

Sandra Cisneros writes with **passion** about Latino **culture**. Many of her stories are based on memories from her **childhood** in the Latino neighborhoods of Chicago. Cisneros's **audience** can see her **commitment** to her culture in the loving way she writes about the Latino way of life.

_____ 1. passion      a. customs and ways of life of a people

_____ 2. culture      b. readers or following

_____ 3. childhood      c. loyalty

_____ 4. audience      d. time of being a child

_____ 5. commitment      e. strong feeling

conflict
influences
poems
relatives
tradition

Sandra Cisneros is a strong and independent woman. In order to become independent, she had to go against some of the **traditions** of her parents and other **relatives**. The **conflict** of breaking away from these early **influences** is the subject of some of her stories and **poems**.

_____ 6. tradition      f. family members

_____ 7. relatives      g. pieces of writing that rhyme

_____ 8. conflict      h. things that have an effect on others

_____ 9. influences      i. disagreement

_____ 10. poems      j. ways of life handed down from parents to children

**Instructor's Notes:** Read aloud the instructions and the words in color. Have students read the paragraphs and complete the exercises. Then discuss the clues that helped them match the words and definitions.

11

# Vocabulary: Multiple Meanings

A word can have more than one meaning. To decide which meaning fits the sentence you are reading, look at the words surrounding it. Think about how the word is used in the sentence.

Look at four different meanings for *border*:

a. the edge of an area
b. a line that separates countries or states
c. a design around the edge of something
d. to be close to

**A. Write the letter of the meaning that best fits the way *border* is used in these sentences.**

_____ 1. Our front yard borders on the playground.

_____ 2. You need the right papers to cross the border between Mexico and the United States.

_____ 3. The book jacket had a pretty pattern for a border.

_____ 4. These lines mark the borders of the playing field.

Look at four different meanings for *hard*:

a. firm to the touch
b. difficult
c. unfeeling
d. with great effort

**B. Write the letter of the meaning that best fits the way *hard* is used in these sentences.**

_____ 1. Yesterday's assignment was hard.

_____ 2. She pushed the car as hard as she could.

_____ 3. He fell on the hard pavement.

_____ 4. Mr. Smith is a hard man.

**Instructor's Notes:** Read the instructions and definitions with students. After they complete the exercises, have them use different meanings of the words in their own sentences.

# Word Study: Dividing Words into Syllables—The VCCV Pattern

You can divide a word into parts called **syllables**. This can help you figure out how to read the word. To tell how many syllables a word has, count the vowel sounds. Each syllable has a vowel sound.

Each of these words has two vowel sounds and two syllables. The / divides the syllables.

thir/teen    pen/cil    pat/tern    pub/lish    cus/tom

The letters on either side of the / follow a pattern. The first vowel in each word is followed by two consonants and then another vowel. The pattern is this: **VC/CV**. Divide the word into syllables between the two consonants.

| VC CV | VC CV | VC CV | VC CV | VC CV |
|---|---|---|---|---|
| thir/teen | pen/cil | pat/tern | pub/lish | cus/tom |

**Read each sentence. Use what you know about sounds, syllables, and sentence meaning to figure out what the underlined word means. Write the underlined word in syllables. Then circle the meaning.**

1. Cisneros has great <u>appeal</u> for many types of readers.

   _____

   apple      interest      words

2. A writer's culture shapes his or her <u>viewpoint</u>.

   _____

   way of looking at life      ability to see      intelligence

3. Cisneros had to <u>struggle</u> to become comfortable in two worlds. _____

   write      work hard      give in

4. A poet such as Cisneros can use words to <u>affect</u> her readers in different ways. _____

   prepare      move      stop

**Instructor's Notes:** Review the explanation of syllables with students. Make sure students understand that there is a vowel sound in each syllable of a word.

## BACK TO THE STORY

▪▪▪▪▪▪▪▪▪▪ **Remember:** What kind of conflict does Sandra Cisneros write about?
▪▪▪▪▪▪▪▪▪▪ **Predict:** Look at the map. What are the homelands of Latinos in the U.S.A.?

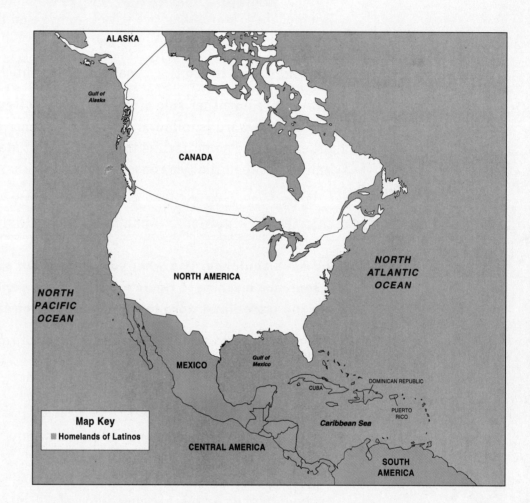

# One Woman, Two Worlds

The people in Sandra Cisneros's stories live in two worlds. Some of her characters live in Mexico. Others live in the United States. But they all think about life *en el otro lado* (on the other side).

**Instructor's Notes:** Discuss the map. Have students read silently. Then invite them to discuss their reactions to the two Cisneros stories.

Here are two examples:

- The story "Woman Hollering Creek" is about a young Mexican woman. She moves to Texas to marry a Mexican-American. She's glad to leave her father and his old ways behind. She expects her life in the United States to be romantic and pleasant. But her husband is not a kind man. Her life is not what she had hoped. She is very unhappy. Finally she gets the courage to move back to her father's house *en el otro lado*.

- In "Remember the Alamo," a Mexican dancer named Tristen wins fame in a San Antonio nightclub. Mexican-Americans flock there to watch him. He reminds them of all they left behind *en el otro lado*.

### Reaching a Large Audience

Sandra Cisneros hopes her success will help other Latina writers. She believes Latinos in the U.S have important stories to tell. As you can see by the graph, about thirteen and a half million Americans are of Mexican origin. But the U.S. has few well-known Latino writers.

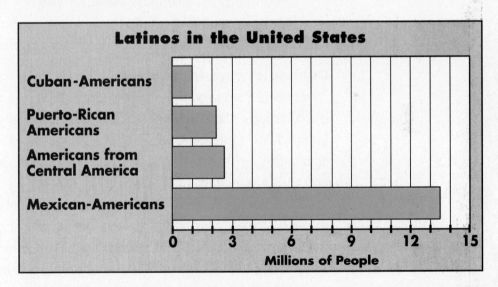

Cisneros's stories appeal to U.S. Latino audiences with roots in many countries. Non-Latinos also enjoy Cisneros's stories. Like all good writers, Cisneros writes about experiences and feelings everyone knows. Many of her stories are about the powerful memories we all have of our own childhood and teenage years.

### Using Memories

Many stories start out as memories. These tales about growing up give readers a sense of life in some special time and place. Cisneros often writes about growing up in Chicago in the 1960s. She remembers what it's like to be a small child. She remembers how it feels to believe you're ugly or powerless, or to feel sad, angry, lonely, or puzzled.

Cisneros also relives the fun of childhood in her stories.

- In the story "Barbie Q," two children go to a flea market. They can't afford to buy new toys. At the market they find toys from a warehouse that burned down. These toys are very cheap. The children buy Barbie Doll clothes that will always smell like smoke and ashes. The children don't mind the smell. They are happy with their treasures.

- "Mexican Movies" is a short, simple story. Cisneros tells about the fun of going to a Mexican movie. The movie itself is not the main attraction. The children at the movie like the popcorn, the coin machines, running up and down the aisles, and being with relatives and friends.

When they read stories like these, many readers think: "I remember something almost exactly like that from my childhood!"

### Coming of Age in America

Growing up is not easy. To grow up, people must often learn hard lessons about life. Most people have memories of when they learned life's hard lessons. Stories about these memories are called coming-of-age stories. You come of age when an experience helps you to mature.

The U.S. is home to people of many cultures. For children of other cultures, coming of age can be hard. Many American writers with roots in other countries have written coming-of-age stories. They write about coping with strange languages and customs. They write about deciding whether to take on new ways or to keep the old ones.

As you recall, in her stories and poems Sandra Cisneros deals with the conflict between cultures. The same conflict has been faced by thousands of Americans. Here are some writers who have told about this conflict as it took place in their own lives:

- Frederick Douglass in his *Autobiography*
- Mary Antin in *The Promised Land*
- Richard Wright in *Native Son*
- Maxine Hong Kingston in *Women Warriors*
- Maya Angelou in *I Know Why the Caged Bird Sings*
- Peri Thomas in *Down These Mean Streets*

## Meeting the Challenge of Writing

Turning memories of the past into good stories takes hard work. Like all good writers, Cisneros seems to follow certain tried and true rules.

1. Keep it simple. Tell your story directly.
2. When you believe in an idea or a way of life, let your story show your commitment. Passionate writing influences the reader's heart and mind.
3. Use language in a creative way. Think of word patterns and images that reflect life as you see it.

Here's how one of Cisneros's story characters describes a very common feeling:

"Rachel says that love is like a big black piano being pushed off the top of a three-story building and you're waiting at the bottom to catch it."

Cisneros blends images like these with a deep love of Latino culture. Her passion and her fierce, sharp honesty give her stories and poems their power. Her work has been called "sensitive" and "quick-witted." One book reviewer says:

"Sandra Cisneros knows both that the heart can be broken and that it can rise and soar like a bird. Whatever story she chooses to tell, we should be listening for a long time to come."

## Comprehension

### Think About It

1. How does Sandra Cisneros put her own life experiences to work?
2. Who are some of the characters in her stories?
3. What is a coming-of-age story?
4. Sum up the reasons why Cisneros's stories and poems appeal to a wide audience.

### Write About It

What memories do you have of your childhood? What event could you include in a real-life story?

**Instructor's Notes:** Have students read and answer the questions. **Write About It** can be used as a writing or discussion assignment.

# Comprehension: Recalling Facts

**Choose the best answer to each question. Fill in the circle.**

1. Where was Sandra Cisneros born?

   ○ **a.** in Mexico
   ○ **b.** in Illinois
   ○ **c.** in Texas

2. What is Cisneros's cultural background?

   ○ **a.** Puerto Rican
   ○ **b.** Dominican
   ○ **c.** Mexican American

3. To what city did Cisneros move as an adult?

   ○ **a.** San Antonio
   ○ **b.** New York
   ○ **c.** Chicago

4. What decision did Cisneros make when she grew up?

   ○ **a.** to live independently
   ○ **b.** to get married
   ○ **c.** to become a lawyer

5. What is the subject of many of Cisneros's stories?

   ○ **a.** traveling
   ○ **b.** growing up
   ○ **c.** earning money

6. To whom do Cisneros's stories and poems appeal?

   ○ **a.** just Latinos
   ○ **b.** mainly women
   ○ **c.** a wide audience

**Instructor's Notes:** Read the instructions with students. After students complete the exercises, review the answers.

# Comprehension: Character Traits

When you read a story by Sandra Cisneros, you meet people with distinct character traits. A **character trait** is a way of behaving or acting that is typical of a specific person. Character traits are what make individuals unique and recognizable.

**How To Identify Character Traits:**

1. Read the paragraph, story, or article carefully.

2. As you read, jot down phrases or words that give clues about how the person acts.

3. Look for actions and thought patterns that the person repeats over a long period of time.

**A. Read the paragraph below to identify Leon's character traits.**

We were all standing around wondering how to get the fallen tree off the house. Leon approached with his usual happy swagger. No matter what the problem, he always said he could solve it. But naturally, when Leon saw the size of that tree, he went into his predictable routine. He said he had an errand to do and would be back in a few minutes. Of course, he never showed up. As usual, we got the job done without him.

**B. Fill in the circle for each character trait that fits Leon.**

○ 1. energetic
○ 2. boastful
○ 3. lazy
○ 4. cruel

**Answer:** Traits 2 and 3 fit Leon. The third sentence gives a clue to his boastfulness. The last three sentences show Leon backing away from a big job.

**Instructor's Notes:** Discuss the tips with students. Read together the directions for the exercises and discuss the answer and explanation in **B**. Have students describe a character in their journals.

# Comprehension: Character Traits

**Read the paragraphs. Then fill in the circles for the words that identify the person's character traits.**

A.  Amy signed up for a writing workshop that met three nights a week. She had hundreds of story ideas, and she wanted to explore ways of getting them down on paper. Her roommate couldn't believe it when she heard about the workshop.

"Honestly, Amy," she said. "How are you going to find time to do that, with a full-time job and a dance class every weekend?"

Amy smiled. "Like I usually do," she said. "I just juggle my schedule and fit it all in. Life is too exciting to let opportunities pass me by."

Amy is:

○  1. ambitious
○  2. nervous
○  3. confused
○  4. enthusiastic

B.  Henry took one look at the little kid and knew exactly how the child felt. He was sitting all alone on the stoop, watching the other kids playing kick-the-can. This kid was just a little too skinny and a little too shy to get involved in something competitive. Henry remembered feeling like that when he was little. "Hey, kid!" said Henry. "Catch!" He threw the boy the new softball he'd just found in the park. "And you can keep it," he hollered, as the delighted child caught the ball.

Henry is:

○  1. foolish
○  2. generous
○  3. aware
○  4. suspicious

**Instructor's Notes:** Point out that the instructions apply to both A and B. Discuss students' responses and have them identify sentences and phrases that support their choices.

# Language: Using Adjectives

An **adjective** is a word that describes a person, place, or thing. Adjectives tell what kind, how many, or which. Adjectives are often used before nouns or after linking verbs such as *be*, *become*, *remain*, and *seem*. In the example sentences, each adjective is underlined. An arrow points to the word the adjective describes.

**Examples:** Sandra Cisneros writes <u>powerful</u> stories. (what kind?)

Her book of poems has a <u>red</u> cover. (which?)

She has written <u>numerous</u> short stories. (how many?)

**A. Read each sentence. Draw a line under each adjective. Draw an arrow to the word each adjective describes.**

1. Cisneros has won important awards for her original work.

2. Poems by Cisneros can be funny and sad.

3. The first poems she wrote were published in 1980 as part of a special series.

4. Although it is a major form of communication, writing is an independent and lonely task.

**B. Write your own sentences using these adjectives.**

1. romantic_____

_____

2. humorous_____

_____

3. unforgettable _____

_____

**Instructor's Notes:** Read the definition of an adjective aloud and discuss the examples. Check the sentences that students write.

Would you like to read some of the stories and poems that Sandra Cisneros has written? You'll find books of her short stories, such as *The House on Mango Street*, and volumes of her poetry, such as *My Wicked Wicked Ways*, in your local library. To locate the books and other library materials, you need to become familiar with how a public library is organized.

Books of **fiction** are in one area of the library. These books contain stories with imaginary characters and events. *The House on Mango Street* would be found in the fiction section. Other forms of literature, such as poetry and plays, are usually on separate shelves. Books that contain facts or information are called **nonfiction** and are kept in another part of the library. If you wanted to read a magazine or news story about Sandra Cisneros, you might look in the section called **periodicals**. If your library has records, tapes, CD's, or books on tape, they are stored in a separate area.

To find out if the library has the book you want, check in the library **catalog**. It lists every book the library owns and tells where to find it. You can also ask the **librarian** who is on duty to help you find things.

**Write the correct word to complete each sentence below.**

librarian     fiction     periodicals     nonfiction     catalog

1. Hector looked in the _____ to find out if the library had the book he wanted.

2. *Caramelo*, the novel that Cisneros is working on, will be

   kept on the _____ shelves because it is not a true story.

3. You can find books about how to write a story in the

   _____ section.

4. Look for an article about Cisneros in *The New York Times*

   in the _____ section.

5. The _____ helps people find what they want.

**Instructor's Notes:** Discuss the parts of a library with students. Encourage them to visit a local library to learn about libraries firsthand. Use the Unit Review on page 120 to conclude the unit. Then assign *Reading for Today Workbook Six*, Unit 1.

# If We Had No Constitution

## DISCUSSION

### Remember

Look at the picture. What do you think is happening? Have you ever done this?

### Predict

Look at the picture and the story title. What do you think this story is about?

**Instructor's Notes:** Read the discussion questions with students. Discuss the story title and the situation in the photo. Introduce the word *Constitution* and explain that it is the document that sets out the principles of American government. Ask students if they have heard the term *constitutional rights*.

Your life is touched by words written over 200 years ago—the United States Constitution. What would life be like without it?

Gary Stahl turned off the TV in disgust. "Why is it that every time I can watch TV, there's nothing good on?" he growled.

"What's the matter?" asked Rosa, his wife. "You have 23 channels to choose from. Surely you can find something to watch."

"Well, I like to watch the woman on the weather channel!" Gary teased. "Everyone else is trying to get me to vote for them in some election. Big deal! What's so great about voting! What does it have to do with me?"

"You're just in a bad mood because you quit smoking again," said Rosa.

"You're a big help," Gary said. "I watch TV for fun, and all I get lately is 'vote for Joe Blow' or 'exercise your constitutional right to vote.' I ask for a little comfort, and you give me a hard time."

"Come on. Let's go for a walk. Then maybe you can forget about voting and that boring old constitutional stuff."

Let's walk with Rosa and Gary. In just a few blocks, they'll come face to face many times with rights that come from our Constitution.

## Results of the Constitution

First, if we had no Constitution, Rosa and Gary might not be here at all. Gary's family came to the United States over 100 years ago. Rosa came from Mexico fifteen years ago. She became a United States citizen six years ago. The Constitution lets people from other countries become citizens of the United States.

Gary and Rosa wave to their neighbor, Helen Sharp, as she leaves for work. Helen wears the uniform of a U.S. Air Force sergeant. She enlisted twelve years ago and gets satisfaction from military life. If there were no Constitution, our country would have no army, navy, or air force to protect us.

**Instructor's Notes:** Have students read the next two pages silently. Have them underline words they don't recognize. Review the underlined words.

Dave Brown, the letter carrier, walks down the street. He has a letter for Rosa from her family in Mexico. Rosa writes to her family often. In the U.S., stamps cost very little and letters arrive quickly. Without the Constitution, we wouldn't even have the United States mail service.

Gary and Rosa notice that a neighbor down the street has a new car. It's the same sporty model they hope to buy next year. The car comes from a factory in another state. Without our Constitution, you might not be able to buy a car made in another state. The Constitution says that the national government should control trade between states. States cannot pass a law to keep out goods that were made in other states.

Two churches are at the corner. One is the church that Rosa attends. Gary sometimes goes to the other, but more often he stays home. If there were no Constitution, we might have only one kind of church in the whole country. And all citizens might have to attend whether they wanted to or not.

Gary and Rosa stop at the grocery store to cool off and buy a soft drink. Once again our Constitution affects what they buy and how they pay for it. Without the Constitution, we wouldn't have one system of money for all the states. Or worse, the soft drinks might not be safe to drink. Under the Constitution, our government makes sure that all foods sold to the public are safe.

As Rosa and Gary walk near the main square, they see many cars parked around it. The county judge is hearing an important court case today. Some of the cars belong to people who will be witnesses in the case. If there were no Constitution, people charged with crimes might not get a fair hearing. Judges might hold secret hearings. And people charged with crimes might not be able to have witnesses tell their side of the story.

# Vocabulary: Definitions

**Read each paragraph below. Notice how the other words in each sentence help define the new word. Match the vocabulary words with their meanings. Write the letter.**

amendments
Constitution
democracy
document
guarantee

The **Constitution** is the basic plan of government for the United States of America. This short **document**, only four pages long, sets up a form of government called a **democracy**. At the time the Constitution was written, most nations were ruled by kings. Over the years, a number of **amendments** have been added to the Constitution. These amendments help **guarantee** our rights.

_____ 1. Constitution     a. changes

_____ 2. document     b. make sure of

_____ 3. democracy     c. basic laws of the U.S.

_____ 4. amendments     d. official paper

_____ 5. guarantee     e. form of government in which citizens elect lawmakers

accused
convicted
illegal
testify
warrant

The rights of people **accused** of crimes are among the most important rights in the Constitution. For example, a person cannot be **convicted** of a crime without a fair hearing. It is **illegal** for the police to search someone's home without a **warrant**. Another important right is the right to say nothing. A person accused of a crime does not have to **testify** about facts that might help a jury convict him or her.

_____ 6. accused     f. found guilty

_____ 7. convicted     g. tell what one knows

_____ 8. illegal     h. charged with breaking the law

_____ 9. warrant     i. against the law; not legal

_____ 10. testify     j. written order allowing police to search a home or business

**Instructor's Notes:** Read aloud the instructions and the words in color. Have students read the paragraphs and complete the exercises. Then discuss the clues that helped them match the words and definitions.

# Vocabulary: Word Stress

The word pairs below look alike. But they are pronounced differently and have different meanings.

**A. Read each word, putting stress or emphasis on the syllable in dark type. Then read the meaning of each word.**

1. a. **con**vict—a person in prison
   b. con**vict**—find guilty
2. a. **ref**use—trash
   b. re**fuse**—won't do, say no
3. a. **ob**ject—an item
   b. ob**ject**—give an opposing opinion
4. a. **con**tent—what is inside
   b. con**tent**—happy, satisfied
5. a. **min**ute—sixty seconds
   b. mi**nute**—tiny
6. a. **reb**el—one who fights against
   b. re**bel**—fight against

**B. Read each sentence. When you see a word from the list above, write *a* or *b* to show which meaning is used in the sentence. Then circle the syllable to stress.**

_____ 1. Because of Benjamin Franklin's age and poor health, four convicts had to carry him into the State house.

_____ 2. Sixteen writers of the Constitution refused to sign it.

_____ 3. Why did they object to it? They thought it gave the national government too much power.

_____ 4. After the Constitution was made public, citizens studied its content carefully.

_____ 5. They read each minute detail with interest.

_____ 6. In 1787 many British people still thought of Americans as rebels.

_____ 7. Americans rebelled against British rule in 1775.

**Instructor's Notes:** For A, review with students the pronunciations and definitions of the word pairs. For B, review the directions and have students complete the exercise. Then have students read the sentences aloud, pronouncing the words with the stresses they have marked.

# Word Study: Dividing Words into Syllables—The VCV Pattern

When you divide words into syllables, you look for vowel and consonant patterns. Many words have the **VCV** pattern shown here:

| VCV | VCV | VCV | VCV |
|---|---|---|---|
| basic | travel | amend | closet |

| VCV | VCV | VCV | VCV |
|---|---|---|---|
| above | legal | lemon | aware |

**Tips for Dividing VCV Words**

When you divide **VCV** words into syllables, use these guidelines:
- If the first vowel sound is <u>long</u> or has the <u>schwa</u> sound, you usually divide the word after the first vowel.
  **Examples:** ba/sic  a/mend
- If the first vowel sound is <u>short</u>, you usually divide the word after the consonant.
  **Example:** lem/on

**A. Read the words in color aloud, listening to the first vowel sound in each one. Write the words on the correct lines below. Then divide the words into syllables by drawing a slash line between the syllables.**

1. The first vowel sound is long. _____

2. The first vowel sound is the schwa. _____

3. The first vowel sound is short. _____

**B. Read the words below aloud. Divide them into syllables.**

1. second _____   2. notice _____

3. modern _____   4. image _____

5. obey _____   6. again _____

7. alarm _____   8. limit _____

**BACK TO THE STORY**

■■■■■■■■■ **Remember:** What have you learned about the Constitution so far?

■■■■■■■■■ **Predict:** Look at the three subheads. What do you think you will learn in the rest of the article?

# If We Had No Constitution

Our Constitution was written over 200 years ago. Since then, the American people have voted to amend, or change, this important document only 26 times. How can we explain this surprisingly small number of amendments? Has America changed so very little in the last 200 years? Or did the writers of the Constitution write a document so thorough and complete that it requires little amendment?

To find the answer, let's look at what America and Americans were like in 1787. We'll take another walk ... this time through the past to Philadelphia, the largest city in the new nation.

It's hot this summer of 1787. The United States has been free of British rule for four years. A group of 55 leading citizens meet inside a building they call the State House. In spite of the heat, they must close the windows to keep out the flies. Without the relief of modern air conditioning, the room feels like a steam bath.

It's noisy, too. The streets outside have a stone surface. The wheels of passing wagons make such a terrific racket that the writers have trouble concentrating. The noise becomes so annoying that workers spread dirt on the streets to muffle the clatter.

Children play marbles in the dirt outside. A stand on the corner sells steaming bowls of pepper pot—a stew of beef, potatoes, and peppers. Women in long dresses stroll by. Their hair is piled high beneath their fancy hats.

A barefoot boy in knee pants sells newspapers on the corner. The paper has a story about a woman whose neighbors attacked her because they believed she was a witch. An ad gives notice that the stage traveling from Philadelphia to New York leaves daily at three o'clock. Mr. John Jones advertises the sale of smoked meat to the public. A man and woman buy a paper. Then they stop at a bookstore

**Instructor's Notes:** Read the questions with students. Help students review and predict. Have students read silently.

to buy a new book for their children. Its title is *The History of Little Goody Twoshoes.*

In his office down the street, a doctor puts leeches on a woman's arm to relieve her headaches. In another office nearby, a dentist has just bought the perfectly good front teeth of a man. After he pulls them, the dentist will use the good teeth to make a set of false teeth for anther patient.

In 1787 much of Philadelphia's daily activity revolves around the city's port. Down on Front Street, 200 docks reach into the Delaware River. Nearly 300 ships crowd the harbor. Along Market Street, merchants sell their goods in open-air stalls. Cooks quickly snap up fresh meats and vegetables. People must buy food every day because there are no refrigerators.

## A Constitution Is Written

Often, the sound of angry voices comes from inside the State House. Benjamin Franklin, popular for his sense of humor, is the peace keeper. "We come to confer, not to contend," Franklin reminds the group. He is 81 years old and so ill that four convicts must carry him into each meeting. The frustrated voices grow quieter as the group listens to Franklin's advice.

The writers argue about almost everything. Calm dialogue breaks down into heated argument. The meetings go on for five hours a day, six days a week, week after week. Everything that happens inside the room is kept secret. One man, James Madison, takes notes, but 50 years will pass before the public will see them. The citizens of Philadelphia wonder what's happening inside the State House, but no one will tell.

Some members of the group become angry and leave. Some never return. On several occasions the group nearly quits. But the writers persist until they work out each problem to the satisfaction of the group. Finally their determination pays off. On September 17, 1787, America's 39 founding fathers sign the Constitution. At last, citizens see the new plan for their American government. They examine the document's content carefully.

Today few Americans ever read the Constitution word for word. But you probably know the basic content of the democracy it guarantees. In a democracy, the people rule themselves. No kings or political groups control the citizens. Everyone has the opportunity to voice any opinion without fear of being punished.

Our Constitution recognizes one government for the whole country, but it divides political power between the states and the nation. Some powers belong only to the national government, some only to the states, and some to both. Congress makes the laws. The president carries out the laws. The Supreme (highest) Court decides if laws are fair.

## A Living Document

Few of the writers expected the Constitution to go unchanged for very long. They knew that the nation would grow, and people would amend the Constitution to meet their needs.

However, the writers of the Constitution were wiser than most people. They built a way of changing the Constitution into the document itself. Americans have amended the Constitution 26 times since 1787. The first ten amendments, the Bill of Rights, were added in 1791.

The Bill of Rights guarantees you certain personal freedoms and prevents the government from interfering with your rights. Some of these are the freedom of speech, freedom of the press, and the right to vote. The Bill of Rights also says that no one may search your home or possessions without a warrant. The courts cannot try you twice for the same crime. You cannot be forced to testify against yourself in court. And you cannot be held in jail for unusually high bail.

If there is doubt about a person's rights, the Supreme Court decides. The Court's findings help to make the Constitution a living document. As America changes, the Supreme Court makes sure that the Constitution doesn't get out of date.

## Court Decisions That Affect Your Life

Over the years, many ordinary people like you have become famous as a result of Supreme Court cases. Here are a few of the Supreme Court's most important decisions. Let's examine how they still affect our lives today.

*Gibbons v. Ogden (1824).* The state of New York gave Aaron Ogden a permit to run a steamboat between New York City and

New Jersey. The United States gave Thomas Gibbons a permit to do the same. Ogden sued Gibbons. The Supreme Court ruled that Congress, not the states, has the right to control trade and travel between states. Gibbons could run his steamboat.

**What It Means to You:** The Supreme Court's decision means that today, you can travel freely from one state to another. If each state controlled trade and travel, you might have to pay to go from Ohio to Indiana.

*Mapp v. Ohio (1961).* Police banged on Dollree Mapp's door. They were looking for a man suspected of setting off a bomb. Mapp refused to let them in. The police broke in and searched her home without a warrant. They found proof that she had broken a law, and Mapp went to prison. The Supreme Court ruled that it was illegal for the police to search Mapp's home without a warrant. She was released from jail.

**What It Means to You:** You don't have to let police search your home without a warrant. The Fourth Amendment to the Constitution guarantees you this right. Police cannot use information from an illegal search to convict you of a crime.

*Gideon v. Wainwright (1961).* The police arrested Clarence Gideon for stealing. He asked the judge to give him a lawyer. The judge did not. Gideon was convicted in court and sent to jail. Gideon wrote to the Supreme Court. The Court ruled that he must get a new hearing, this time with a lawyer to help him. At his second hearing, the court found Gideon innocent.

**What It Means to You:** If you are accused of a crime, you have the right to a lawyer. Even if you don't want a lawyer, the judge may give you one if your case is serious.

*Miranda v. Arizona (1966).* Police questioned Ernesto Miranda for two hours before he admitted to a crime. They didn't tell Miranda about the Fifth Amendment to the Constitution. This amendment guarantees that a person accused of a crime cannot be forced to testify against himself or herself. The Supreme Court ruled that Miranda should have a new hearing.

**What It Means to You:** If the police arrest you for a crime, they will read you these words: "You have the right to remain silent. Anything you say can and will be used against you in a court of law. You have the right to a lawyer. If you cannot afford a lawyer, one will be provided for you. You have the right to have a lawyer present during questioning. You have the right to end questioning at any time."

*Harper v. Virginia State Board of Education (1966).* Many states once required people to pay a tax before they could vote. This tax often kept poor people from voting. In 1964 the Twenty-Fourth Amendment to the Constitution struck down the tax in national elections. Two years later the Supreme Court ruled that making people pay a tax to vote in state elections is illegal.

**What It Means to You:** This ruling guarantees you the right to vote without having to pay a tax. In general, you must be a citizen of the United States and be 18 years of age or older to vote.

The four sheets of paper on which the Constitution is written are old. But the ideas are still as fresh and new as the day they were written. The main ideas are simple. Government gets its power from the people. People have rights that the government cannot change. The people have the right to make the laws. Government must obey the laws.

Democracy, more than a form of government, is a way of life. Imagine how different your life would be if these freedoms had not been preserved in the Constitution that hot summer of 1787.

# Comprehension

## Think About It

1. Why is the Constitution important to Americans?
2. How is the Constitution changed?
3. How does the Supreme Court affect the Constitution?
4. Sum up the important points of the article.

## Write About It

How do you feel about the rights guaranteed to you in the Constitution? Describe what they mean to you.

**Instructor's Notes:** Have students read and answer the questions. **Write About It** can be used as a writing or discussion assignment.

# Comprehension: Recalling Facts/Main Idea

**A. Choose the best answer to each question. Fill in the circle.**

1. Under the Constitution, who makes the laws we follow?

    ○ **a.** the President
    ○ **b.** the Congress
    ○ **c.** the Supreme Court

2. When did the founding fathers sign the Constitution?

    ○ **a.** September 17, 1787
    ○ **b.** 1791
    ○ **c.** during the hot summer of 1787

**B. Choose the sentence that best states the main idea. Fill in the circle.**

1. The main point of the Supreme Court's ruling in *Mapp v. Ohio* is

    ○ **a.** Dollree Mapp chose the wrong kind of people as friends.
    ○ **b.** The police cannot search your home without a warrant.
    ○ **c.** Setting off a bomb is a very serious crime.

2. The main point of the Supreme Court's ruling in *Miranda v. Arizona* is

    ○ **a.** Questioning a suspect for more than one hour is illegal.
    ○ **b.** Some police officers refuse to follow the Fourth Amendment.
    ○ **c.** People accused of a crime can't be forced to testify against themselves.

3. The main point of the Supreme Court's ruling in *Harper v. Virginia State Board of Education* is

    ○ **a.** No government can tax a citizen's right to vote.
    ○ **b.** Only U.S. citizens age 18 or older can vote.
    ○ **c.** Poor people shouldn't vote because they probably don't understand the issues.

**Instructor's Notes:** For A, remind students that the words *who* and *when* call for facts. For B, review
|the information about finding the main idea from *Reading for Today Book Four*, Units 3 and 4. After students
complete the exercises, review the answers.

# Comprehension: Cause and Effect

A **cause** is a person, thing, or situation that produces a result. The cause answers the question **Why**? An effect is the outcome that results from a cause. An **effect** answers the question **What happened**?

---

**How To Find Cause and Effect:**

1. Read the sentence, paragraph, or story carefully.

2. List the facts. Look for places where one fact follows another. Ask yourself: *Do these facts simply show a sequence of events? Or do the facts show cause and effect?*

3. Look for cause words such as *the reason for, because, caused by, since*, and *why*.

4. Look for effect words such as *the product, the result, the outcome, so*, and *the consequence*.

---

**A. Read the sentence below and find the cause. Fill in the circle.**

In 1787 cooks shopped for food every day

- ○ 1. and then went home.
- ○ 2. because no one had a refrigerator.
- ○ 3. during the coolest part of the day.

**Answer:** Choice 2 has the clue word *because*. Choice 1 is wrong because it describes the sequence of events, not the cause. Choice 3 is wrong because it answers the question *when*, not *why*.

**B. Read the sentence below and find the effect. Fill in the circle.**

Some citizens were afraid the strange woman was a witch

- ○ 1. so they attacked her.
- ○ 2. since she talked to herself.
- ○ 3. who had special powers.

**Answer:** Choice 1 has the clue word *so*. Choice 2 is a cause, not an effect. Choice 3 only describes the woman.

---

**36** **Instructor's Notes:** Discuss the tips with students. Read together the directions for the exercises and discuss the answers and explanations. Have students write a paragraph showing cause and effect in their journals.

# Comprehension: Cause and Effect

**A. Each phrase states a cause. Fill in the circle for the effect.**

1. The tax on voting rights

   ○ **a.** was passed in 1787.
   ○ **b.** resulted in poor people not voting.
   ○ **c.** is illegal.

2. The people in the State House complained of the noise

   ○ **a.** so dirt was spread on the street.
   ○ **b.** and the heat.
   ○ **c.** in the letters they wrote home to their families.

3. The writers of the Constitution expected changes would be needed through the years

   ○ **a.** so they built in a way to amend it.
   ○ **b.** to keep women from voting.
   ○ **c.** in case our country ever went to war again.

**B. Each phrase states an effect. Fill in the circle for the cause.**

1. The police broke into Dollree Mapp's home

   ○ **a.** and arrested her.
   ○ **b.** because they were looking for a suspect.
   ○ **c.** after they got a search warrant.

2. Democracy is a popular form of government

   ○ **a.** because people like to rule themselves.
   ○ **b.** but it's not practical.
   ○ **c.** especially in Communist countries.

3. The streets of Philadelphia were very noisy

   ○ **a.** and dirty.
   ○ **b.** when children were playing nearby.
   ○ **c.** because wagon wheels clattered on the paved streets.

**Instructor's Notes:** Review with students the steps to determine cause/effect relationships on page 36. After students complete the exercises, review their answers.

# Language: Writing Names and Titles

Use the chart below as a guide when you are writing special names and titles.

| Capitalize the names of: | Examples: |
|---|---|
| • people and their titles | • President George Washington |
| • countries, states, counties, and cities | • America; Pennsylvania; Philadelphia |
| • newspapers, books, and magazines | • *The History of Little Goody Twoshoes* |
| • historic documents and laws | • Constitution of the U.S.; Fourth Amendment |
| • courts of law and other bodies that make laws | • Supreme Court; Congress |
| • streets and buildings | • Front Street; State House |

**Rewrite each sentence using capital letters correctly.**

1. The declaration of independence, written by thomas jefferson in 1776, declared that the american colonies were free of british rule.

   _____

   _____

2. If the constitution were being written today, citizens of philadelphia would read about it in *the philadelphia inquirer*.

   _____

   _____

3. justice sandra day o'connor is the first woman to serve on the united states supreme court.

   _____

   _____

**Instructor's Notes:** Review the chart with students. After students complete the exercise, review their answers.

# Life Skill: Registering To Vote

In a democracy, the people rule themselves. They do this by voting for leaders to represent them. Citizens make their opinions known by voting for representatives who voice these opinions. Therefore, a democracy truly represents the will of the people only if the citizens vote.

One of your most important rights is the right to vote. In 1966, the Supreme Court ruled that placing a tax on voting is illegal. To vote, you must be 18 years or older, be a citizen of the U.S., and live in the county in which you are voting. You must **register**, or enroll, by filling out a voter registration card. Most public libraries and post offices have the cards.

The voter registration card used in your county is similar to the one below. Practice filling out the card.

---

## VOTER REGISTRATION CARD
Please fill out all the information below. Print in ink or type.

| Last Name | First Name | Middle Initial | Maiden Name |
|-----------|-----------|----------------|-------------|
|           |           |                |             |

| Sex | Date of Birth | Telephone # | Social Security # |
|-----|---------------|-------------|-------------------|
|     |               |             |                   |

**Permanent Home Address**

City, State, Zip

**Mailing Address** (if you cannot receive mail at your home address)

City, State, Zip

**I am a citizen of the U.S. and live in this country. I have not been declared mentally unfit in a court of law. I have not been convicted of a felony. I swear that this information is correct. I understand that giving false information to register to vote is a felony.**

_____          _____
Signature of Applicant or Agent                  Relationship of Agent

---

**Instructor's Notes:** Have students read the introduction and complete the voter registration card. Review the completed card. Use the Unit 2 Review on page 121 to conclude the unit. Then assign *Reading for Today Workbook Six*, Unit 2.

# Body Language

*Much of what we mean is seen but not spoken.*

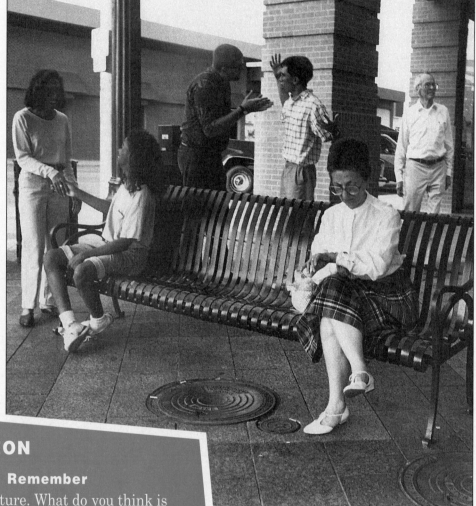

## DISCUSSION

### Remember

Look at the picture. What do you think is happening? What messages are the people communicating?

### Predict

Look at the picture and the title. What do you expect to learn about this topic?

**Instructor's Notes:** Read the discussion questions with students. Discuss the story title, the caption, and the situation in the photo.

Most of us never study it in a book, and yet we are experts at it. We use it all the time. It's so easy to use that we hardly ever think about it. What is it? It's called body language.

We show body language with our eyes, face, arms, and hands. The way we walk, sit, and stand is also part of our body language. As the words of an old song say, "Every little movement has a meaning all its own."

We use some body language on purpose—for a reason. We wave to our friends to signal hello. We nod or shake our heads to signal yes or no. We point to things that catch our attention. When greeting a friend, we may shake hands or hug. Movements such as these usually back up something we are saying.

However, most body language just happens naturally. For example, when people are puzzled or surprised, their eyebrows lift. A yawn goes along with feeling tired or bored. Frowns seem to be a part of worry or anger. Our smiles light up naturally when we are happy or amused.

Words give only part of a message. At least fifty percent, or half, of what a person means comes across in the silent language of the body. Think of body language as an important code. As you learn to read the code, you get to know more about what people are really thinking and feeling. You learn to read people like a book.

**Instructor's Notes:** Have students read the next two pages silently. Have them underline words they don't recognize. Review the underlined words. Discuss the concept of *code*; "a system of signals for sending messages."

At work, many employers are learning the body language code. They read body language to help them judge people who are applying for a job. Body language may help determine who gets hired.

The photo below shows four people who are waiting for a job interview. The employer opens the door, takes one look at them, and comes up with the following ideas. See if you can match each idea with a person in the picture.

1. This one is a "don't get too close" type. This person doesn't want to answer many personal questions. I can tell by the locked arms.

2. That one isn't nervous. That person takes life very easy. I can tell by the way the legs are crossed. That person seems happy just reading and waiting.

3. That one wants to get down to business. That person doesn't like waiting. That one gets bored easily and wants to keep moving.

4. This one could be the thoughtful type. Or maybe the person is just daydreaming.

*While waiting for a job interview, these people tell the employer about themselves through their body language.*

# Vocabulary: Definitions

**Read each paragraph below. Notice how the other words in each sentence help define the new word. Match the vocabulary words with their meanings. Write the letter.**

behavior
facial
gesture
nonverbal
posture

What you say is important, but so is your **behavior**. You may not be aware of every move you make. But, whether you like it or not, your body language sends **nonverbal** messages to other people. A **gesture** such as tightening your fist shows that you are angry. A **facial** movement such as biting your lip shows worry or fear. **Posture** is also a clue to your feelings; standing straight, for example, means you feel proud of yourself.

_____ 1. behavior

_____ 2. nonverbal

_____ 3. gesture

_____ 4. facial

_____ 5. posture

a. movement of a body part to express an idea

b. many ways a person acts or moves

c. without words

d. body stance or position

e. of or about the face

communication
conscious
insight
observe
reveal

When you **observe** body language, you get an **insight** into a person's feelings. Suppose you are talking to a man who is blinking his eyes very fast. This behavior may **reveal** that he is nervous about talking to you. Now that you are **conscious** of his feelings, you can begin to find ways to calm him down. By learning to pick up on nonverbal messages, your **communication** skills improve.

_____ 6. observe

_____ 7. insight

_____ 8. reveal

_____ 9. conscious

_____ 10. communication

f. wisdom and understanding

g. watch carefully

h. exchange of thoughts and ideas

i. make known

j. aware; wide awake to

**Instructor's Notes:** Read aloud the instructions and the words in color. Have students read the paragraphs and complete the exercises. Then discuss the clues that helped them match the words and definitions.

# Vocabulary: Prefixes and Suffixes

A **prefix** is a word part added to the beginning of a word to change the word's meaning. A **suffix** is a word part added to the end of a word to change its function and meaning. Adding a suffix usually changes the part of speech of a word. When you know the meaning of a prefix or suffix, you can often figure out the meaning of a new word.

uncomfortable
unspoken
unconscious
unsure

**A. The prefix *un–* means *not* or *opposite of*. Study the words in color. Choose the correct word for each sentence based on the meaning given.**

1. Some people feel _____ at parties.
   (not at ease)

2. She is _____ of what to say to strangers.
   (not certain)

3. He is _____ of his own body language.
   (not aware)

4. Your behavior is a clue to your _____ messages.
   (not said)

consciousness
nervousness
friendliness
tiredness

**B. The suffix *–ness* means *a state* or *quality*. Study the words in color. Choose the correct word for each sentence based on the meaning given.**

1. Wiggling is a sign of _____ .
   (state of being uneasy)

2. A smile shows _____ .
   (quality of being interested in meeting other people)

3. A sigh can show _____ .
   (state of being weary)

4. Once you understand the code, reading body language

   becomes part of your _____ .
   (state of being aware)

**Instructor's Notes:** Read the definitions of *prefix* and *suffix* with students. After they complete the exercises, have them think of other words with these prefixes and suffixes.

Dividing Words into Syllables
Consonant + *le* Pattern

If you know where to divide a word into syllables, you can usually figure out the vowel sounds in the word.

Some words end in a consonant followed by –*le*.

**Examples:**     table     castle     pickle

---

**Tips for Dividing and Pronouncing Words with –*le***

- The **consonant + *le*** is usually one syllable.
- If a vowel comes before **consonant + *le***, the vowel sound is usually **long**.
  Examples: tā/ble  brī/dle
- If a consonant comes before **consonant + *le***, the vowel sound is usually **short**.
  Examples: căs/tle  căn/dle
- If the word ends in –**ckle**, the –*le* forms the last syllable and the first vowel sound is usually **short**.
  Examples: tăck/le  chŭck/le

---

**Use the tips to divide the words below into syllables. Say the words. Then write each word in a sentence.**

1. purple_____

_____

2. stable_____

_____

3. tickle _____

_____

4. bubble _____

_____

5. cackle_____

_____

**Instructor's Notes:** Read the tips with students. Say the example words aloud and help students identify the short and long vowel sounds. Read the instructions with students and have them complete the exercise.

## BACK TO THE STORY

**Remember:** What have you learned about body language so far?

**Predict:** Look at the picture. What are some other things you think you might learn in this article?

# Body Language

You already have insights into many nonverbal messages that mean *I'm in charge! I'm sure of myself!* The person who walks and stands tall and straight is giving that message. The person with confidence meets your eyes while talking to you. If you're a shy person, remember the stand-tall posture and the direct look. You can consciously do these things. Some shy people report that this conscious behavior makes them feel better about themselves.

Some take-charge body language is so strong that it turns people off. For example, suppose one man visits another man at his office. The visitor sits in the visitor's chair. He leans back with his hands crossed behind his head and puts his feet on the other man's desk. The visitor's posture says, "I'm taking over your space." How would you feel in that situation?

*The finger-wagger may lose an employee or a friend.*

**Instructor's Notes:** Discuss the photo. Have students read silently. Then invite them to share their own observations about body language.

Look at the two pictures on pages 46–47. In each one, a person is taking charge. In one case, the action causes bad feelings. In the other case, the action is pleasant. Compare the use of the hands in each picture.

Here's the behavior of people who feel sure of themselves.
- They stand and walk tall and proud.
- They look you directly in the eye.
- They have a firm handshake.
- If they have good communication skills, they don't yell, point their fingers, or take up your space with their bodies.

Nervous people also reveal their feelings through body language. Their posture is often a clue. They slouch or shift their weight from one foot to the other. They look down or around the room when speaking. Instead of a firm handshake, theirs is cold and limp.

People who feel they are not in control of a situation often show their feelings by really holding on. They may hold their arms

*The speaker's hands show that she feels in control. This gesture doesn't offend people.*

behind their backs and grip their hands together. They may hold the arms of a chair tightly. Or they may fold their arms tightly across their bodies. Each of these postures can mean *I don't feel safe. I'm really trying to hold myself together.*

However, nervous people may reveal their feelings in the opposite way, too. That is, they may move around a great deal. They may wiggle around in the chair. The chair may be comfortable, but the person is not.

Different facial movements also reflect people's tension. People who are unsure of themselves often blink their eyes, lick their lips, or wrinkle their forehead. They may also use some of these gestures: rubbing their forehead, running a finger under the collar, putting a hand to the throat often, or wringing their hands (rubbing them back and forth).

Here's the behavior of people who feel uncomfortable.
- They hold themselves so stiffly that they never seem to move at all.
- Their gestures, posture, and facial expressions always seem to be changing.

## Acting Friendly

Suppose you're at a party with lots of people you've never met before. You feel an attraction for someone you meet. You start to talk to the person. Your smile and posture show your friendliness, but the person turns away. All you can see is a back and a shoulder. Your insight tells you, "This person is giving me the cold shoulder." The body language is very clear. This person is not interested in talking with you, so you don't persist. You move on.

In a social situation, observe what people do with their hands. A tightly-closed hand is nonverbal behavior. It may mean *I'm not telling you anything about myself!* Or it might mean *I'm very shy.* You may want to check the meaning by talking to the person. If the hands open up, the person probably means *I'm ready to share my feelings with you.*

*Her posture shows that she is interested in what he has to say. His posture shows his interest in her. His palms show that he's probably being honest.*

Observe hand-to-mouth gestures. People may put a hand to the mouth for a second just because they are surprised by what you are saying. But other people may hold their hands in front of their mouth while they are speaking. This gesture can mean three different things:

1. *I'm not sure of what I'm saying.*
2. *I'm not telling the truth.*
3. *Let's keep this a secret.*

You can't judge a book by just one sentence. And you can't judge a person by just one gesture or facial expression. You have to add up the person's different physical signals to get the whole picture. For example, a man may look away from a woman for a moment. Does looking away mean that he isn't interested in her? Observe him. Does he quickly straighten his tie and run one hand through his hair? Then he probably is *very* interested! In another moment, he'll turn back and start to talk to her again. Most women, too, unconsciously make the look-away and hair-pat gestures when they're interested in a man.

## Listening to More Than Words

People reveal their feelings through the way they say things. So the way people speak is another part of body language. It's important to know, especially if you can't see the speaker. For example, you can concentrate on the speaker's voice when you're talking on the telephone.

*This speaker's body language isn't clear.*

Someone who is talking very fast could be either nervous or excited. The slow speaker may be very thoughtful or very unsure of what to say next. People who sprinkle their talk with "you know" and "I mean" may be revealing just the opposite. They may not be sure of what they mean. The throat-clearing *ahem* is usually a sign of nervousness. A sigh may reveal worry, boredom, or tiredness.

### How Does It All Add Up?

To communicate well, observe body language and listen to words. On the job or in social situations, people expect your nonverbal messages to match your verbal messages. But very often, a person's behavior and words seem to be communicating different things.

For example, what would you think if your dinner guest tasted the food, frowned, and then commented, "This is really good!" Or suppose you were arguing with a friend about something. Then the other person ended the conversation by yelling, "I'm not mad!" and slammed the door. What's wrong with these situations?

Both speakers are giving mixed messages. These people are not saying what they really mean. In cases like these, we unconsciously look at behavior to get the true meaning of a person's feelings.

To avoid giving mixed messages, try to say what you really mean. Your body language and words match most in situations when you are sure of yourself and sure of the people around you. Then you feel free to show as well as tell what you think. Your nonverbal behavior goes right along with what you're saying. In fact, anyone looking at you might say that you've got it all together!

# Comprehension

## Think About It

1. Why is it helpful to be aware of body language?
2. How do people show that they feel sure of themselves?
3. How do nervous people give themselves away?
4. Sum up what you have learned about body language.

## Write About It

Have you ever been in a situation where reading someone's body language made a big difference? Describe what happened.

**Instructor's Notes:** Have students read and answer the questions. **Write About It** can be used as a writing or discussion assignment.

# Comprehension: Recalling Facts

**A.  Choose the best answer to each question. Fill in the circle.**

1.  Who seems to feel uncomfortable?

    ○  **a.**  the person who stands and walks tall
    ○  **b.**  the person who never looks at you while speaking
    ○  **c.**  the person who looks you directly in the eye

2.  When do people expect your nonverbal messages to match your verbal messages?

    ○  **a.**  only on the job
    ○  **b.**  only in social situations
    ○  **c.**  on the job and in social situations

3.  When would visitors in your office put their feet on your desk?

    ○  **a.**  when they are trying to take over your space
    ○  **b.**  when they have new shoes
    ○  **c.**  when they don't like your shoes

4.  What happens if you learn to read body language?

    ○  **a.**  You are invited to more parties.
    ○  **b.**  Your communication skills improve.
    ○  **c.**  You will get the kind of job you want.

**B.  Read the sentence below. Fill in the circle by the cause.**

People sometimes cover their mouths

○  **a.**  to speak more clearly.
○  **b.**  because they are unsure of what they are saying.
○  **c.**  because they feel certain of themselves.

**C.  Read the sentence below. Fill in the circle by the effect.**

When someone's verbal and nonverbal messages don't match,

○  **a.**  other people get confused.
○  **b.**  other people feel comfortable.
○  **c.**  the communication is clear.

**Instructor's Notes:**  Read the instructions with students. After students complete the exercises, have them identify the correct answers and explain why the other choices are incorrect.

# Comprehension: Inference

An **inference** is a judgment that you make when you combine new information with what you already know. You make an inference by using your thinking skills.

For example, suppose you already know that Carol doesn't like Ted. At a party, Ted tries to talk to Carol. She turns her back to him. From what you have just studied, you know that Carol's body language says "leave me alone." Adding up what you know and what you have studied, you can **infer** that Ted is not going to get Carol's attention.

## How To Make an Inference:

1. Read the paragraph or story. Think about what you read.
2. List the facts that are stated.
3. Put together the stated facts with information you know.
4. Make the inference. (Check yourself by asking if the facts support your thinking.)

**A. Read this paragraph and list the facts.**

Larry greeted Mr. Lorn with a firm handshake. As Larry introduced himself, he looked directly into Mr. Lorn's eyes. Both men were smiling when they sat down.

Fact 1: _____

Fact 2: _____

Fact 3: _____

**B. Which is the best inference to make? Fill in the circle.**

○ 1. Larry's body language shows that he is sure of himself.
○ 2. Larry is a shy person who has trouble during interviews.
○ 3. Mr. Lorn will definitely hire Larry for the job.

**Answer:** Choice 1. Choice 2 is wrong because you know that Larry's body language says, "I feel sure of myself." Choice 3 is wrong because you don't know if Larry is there for a job interview.

**Instructor's Notes:** Discuss the tips with students. Read together the directions for the exercises. Then have students write an inference paragraph in their journals.

# Comprehension: Inference

**A. Read each paragraph and the statements below it. Fill in the circle beside the best inference.**

1. Donna and Mac have just met at a party. They talk for a minute. Then they both turn away. Both pat their hair. Mac fixes his tie. Donna looks sideways at Mac. She smooths her hand over her skirt.

   ○ **a.** Mac is looking for someone else to talk to.
   ○ **b.** Donna doesn't want people to know her.
   ○ **c.** Donna and Mac are interested in each other.

2. The man walks with his shoulders slumped over. He doesn't look at people. When you talk to him, he turns his face away and speaks so softly that you can't understand him.

   ○ **a.** The man has done something wrong.
   ○ **b.** The man is probably shy and troubled.
   ○ **c.** The man is looking for a friend.

**B. Read the paragraph. Answer the questions using complete sentences.**

Mrs. Rown sits behind her desk. She tells May about a new job that she wants May to do. May taps her foot and sighs. She rubs her hand across her forehead. She talks very slowly when she answers Mrs. Rown's questions.

1. What clues does the paragraph give about May's mood?

   _____

   _____

2. What inference can you make about May based on her body language?

   _____

   _____

**Instructor's Notes:** Have students complete the exercises. Then review answers with students. For A, have students identify the correct answers and explain why the other choices are incorrect.

# Language: Writing Complete Sentences

A sentence has two parts. The first part tells *who or what is doing or feeling something*. This first part is called the **subject** of the sentence. The second part of the sentence tells *what is being done or felt*. This part is called the **predicate** of the sentence. The predicate is the verb plus other words that complete the thought. Here are some examples.

| Subject (Noun phrase) | Predicate (Verb phrase) |
|---|---|
| Jean | waved to me. |
| She and I | smiled at each other. |
| Her behavior | revealed her feelings. |
| My friend | is happy. |
| The chair | is comfortable. |

**A. Add a subject to complete each sentence.**

1. _____ studied body language.

2. _____ looked at her friends.

3. _____ bit her lip all the time.

4. _____ felt nervous.

5. _____ is uncomfortable.

6. _____ shook hands firmly.

**B. Add a predicate to complete each sentence.**

1. Tony _____

2. I _____

3. His body language _____

4. A shy person _____

5. All of us _____

**Instructor's Notes:** Review the definition of a sentence with students. Check the sentences that students complete.

# Life Skill: Writing a Summary of Qualifications

Suppose you are applying for a job. You know that your body language is important. Did you know that a good **resume** can be a big help, too? A resume is a written summary of who you are and what your background is. A resume also tells why you are **qualified** for a job. It is a way of selling yourself—making you stand out from all the others.

Here are some highlights from a resume. These qualifications summarize the strengths this person has to offer for a particular job.

| | |
|---|---|
| *Objective:* | Position as a waiter in a good, medium-priced restaurant |
| *Qualifications:* | 2 years experience in a family diner<br>Able to assess and adapt to moods and needs of customers and other staff<br><br>Highly creative in solving problems and getting along with others<br><br>Quick, reliable, and productive<br><br>Well-organized; good at details |

**Think of a job that you would like. Then write five qualifications that you could use on a resume to help you get that job.**

*Objective*: Position as _____

1. _____

2. _____

3. _____

4. _____

5. _____

**Instructor's Notes:** Make sure that students understand what a resume is. Discuss why the sample qualifications for a waiter might help someone get the job. Use the Unit 3 Review on page 122 to conclude the unit. Then assign *Reading for Today Workbook Six*, Unit 3.

# *Amazing Mary*

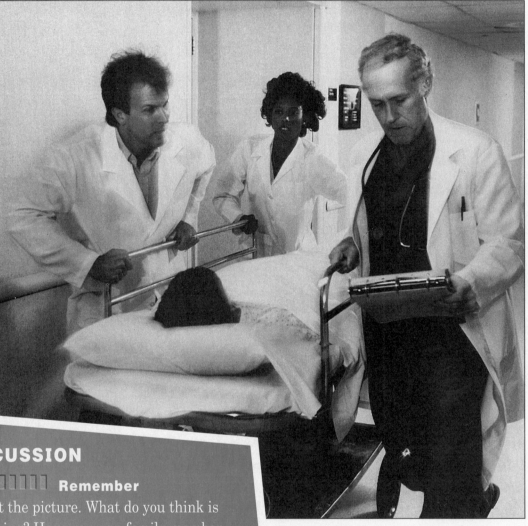

## DISCUSSION

### Remember

Look at the picture. What do you think is happening? Have you or a family member ever been in the hospital?

### Predict

Look at the picture and the story title. What do you think this story is about?

**Instructor's Notes:** Read the discussion questions with students. Discuss the story title, subtitles, and, the photo. Explain that this is a nonfiction selection about a real person.

The twenty-five-year-old woman circled the man on the karate mat, looking for an opening. Holding her arms stretched out before her, she moved her feet carefully. The man crouched low and grabbed at her. She moved with incredible speed, and in an instant the man was on his back. She held his shoulders in a firm grip. Leaning over, she said, "You know, I really like you."

After that first meeting in karate class, Mary Groda spent several weeks trying to get David Lewis interested in her. David didn't know what to think of her. Mary talked about her life, but things she said didn't always go together. She had dropped out of school, but she wanted to be a doctor. She had never been married, but she had two children. She could pin him to the mat in karate class, but she'd had five heart attacks and a stroke. Mary seemed to be a nice person, but she'd been in trouble with the law twice.

Everything Mary told David was true. She was born in San Antonio, Texas, in 1949. She had six brothers and sisters. She came from a poor family. And she was determined to be a doctor.

## Someone From Another Planet

All the odds were against her. Mary never did well in school. "School was a bore," Mary said. Her teachers didn't know that Mary had a problem learning to read and write.

Mary wanted to learn, but she felt out of place in school, like someone from another planet. "I didn't know what they were talking about," she said. She felt frustrated every day that she went to school because she didn't understand what was going on.

But Mary managed to fake her way through school. She pretended to read her books. She also listened carefully and memorized what her teacher said. Sometimes she made up stories about the pictures in her books.

One day Mary had a fight with a boy and broke a finger. She didn't have to write while her finger was mending. Every time the doctor put a cast on her broken finger, Mary ripped it off. Getting a new cast kept her out of school.

**Instructor's Notes:** Have students read the next two pages silently. Have them underline words they don't recognize. Review the underlined words. Check students' recognition of *karate* and *microscope*.

The doctor finally figured out what Mary was doing. He understood her game, so he kept Mary with him while he worked in the hospital. The doctor told Mary about the work he was doing. He let her look through his microscope. "It was his way of keeping me out of trouble," Mary said. "I thought that if I ever became a doctor, he was the sort of doctor I'd want to be."

Mary's family moved to Portland, Oregon, and worked as crop pickers. Picking strawberries was hard work. "You have to break your back getting down to them. You're on your hands and knees all day long. I will not eat strawberries to this day."

Mary kept skipping school. She had to wear used clothes, and other children made fun of her. She felt worthless. "The city kids made us feel ashamed. I went into the streets. That was real life, real learning for me. And the kids there didn't care what I wore."

## Stubborn Mary

Mary started drinking and soon got in trouble with the law. After she was arrested five times, she was sent away to reform school, a place for troublemakers. She stayed there for two years.

When Mary got out, she went to high school. She still didn't know how to read or write, but she knew she wasn't stupid. No one understood why she was frustrated. A rage built inside Mary, and she became more stubborn than ever. "If you said not to do something, that's just what Mary would do," her mother said. "Mary did whatever she wanted."

At sixteen, Mary got into real trouble. Looking for fun, she spent time with a wild crowd. "I ran away in a stolen car with a boy named Jim," Mary said. Police gave chase, and Jim drove wildly over mountain roads. An officer shot out a rear tire. The car slid off the road and 80 feet down into a ditch. Mary and Jim were not hurt, but Mary was sent away again.

# Vocabulary: Definitions

**Read each paragraph below. Notice how the other words in each sentence help define the new word. Match the vocabulary words with their meanings. Write the letter.**

conceal
dedication
physician
sensitive
severe

When Mary arrived at the reform school, she was an angry young woman with **severe** problems. She used her tough reputation to **conceal** the **sensitive** person inside. Only the kind **physician** who had treated Mary's broken finger had understood her. In fact, his **dedication** had given her something to think about.

_____ 1. severe  **a.** giving one's attention to a cause

_____ 2. conceal  **b.** doctor

_____ 3. sensitive  **c.** very serious

_____ 4. physician  **d.** easily hurt

_____ 5. dedication  **e.** hide

assist
disability
overcome
resent
unbearable

Mary's experiences at school left her with feelings that would be hard to **overcome**. "It was **unbearable** to me to be in school," she said. No one there knew how to **assist** her. No one suspected the cause of her reading **disability**. And Mary could only **resent** the people who caused her pain.

_____ 6. overcome  **f.** too painful to put up with

_____ 7. unbearable  **g.** feel angry about

_____ 8. assist  **h.** lack of ability to do something

_____ 9. disability  **i.** get control over; rise above

_____ 10. resent  **j.** help

**Instructor's Notes:** Read aloud the instructions and the words in color. Have students complete the exercises. Then discuss the clues that helped students match the words and definitions.

# Vocabulary: Antonyms

**Antonyms** are words with opposite or nearly opposite meanings. For example, *friend* is the antonym of *enemy*.

**A. Match each vocabulary word with its antonym. Write the letter.**

_____ 1. disability     **a.** reveal; show

_____ 2. sensitive     **b.** mild

_____ 3. conceal     **c.** frustrate; prevent

_____ 4. assist     **d.** unfeeling

_____ 5. severe     **e.** talent; power

_____ 6. overcome     **f.** acceptable; OK

_____ 7. unbearable     **g.** give in to; fail

**B. Write a sentence of your own using each underlined word.**

1. Mary had a reading <u>disability</u>.

_____

2. She broke her finger to <u>conceal</u> her lack of ability to write.

_____

3. The physician who treated Mary <u>prevented</u> her from removing the casts by spending time with her.

_____

4. He was <u>sensitive</u> to her feelings, unlike the children in school.

_____

5. Street life became more <u>acceptable</u> to Mary than going to school. _____

6. Two years in reform school seemed like a <u>severe</u> sentence to Mary. _____

**Instructor's Notes:** Discuss the definition of *antonym* with students. Read each set of directions with students. Encourage students to share their sentences from B.

# Word Study: Dictionary Entries

You can use the dictionary to find out many things about a word. First you learn how to say the word correctly. A dictionary entry shows how many syllables a word has and how to say the vowel and consonant sounds. Next the dictionary shows you how a word acts in a sentence (as a noun, verb, adjective, etc.). Then the entry gives the word meaning. One word may have many meanings. A number (**1**, **2**, **3**) comes before each meaning. Study this dictionary entry for the word *sensitive*.

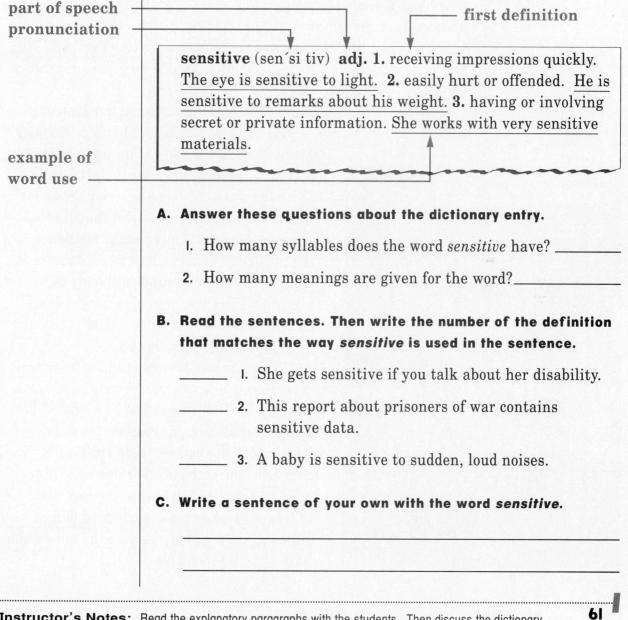

part of speech
pronunciation

first definition

**sensitive** (sen´si tiv) **adj. 1.** receiving impressions quickly. The eye is sensitive to light. **2.** easily hurt or offended. He is sensitive to remarks about his weight. **3.** having or involving secret or private information. She works with very sensitive materials.

example of word use

**A. Answer these questions about the dictionary entry.**

 1. How many syllables does the word *sensitive* have? _____

 2. How many meanings are given for the word?_____

**B. Read the sentences. Then write the number of the definition that matches the way *sensitive* is used in the sentence.**

 _____ 1. She gets sensitive if you talk about her disability.

 _____ 2. This report about prisoners of war contains sensitive data.

 _____ 3. A baby is sensitive to sudden, loud noises.

**C. Write a sentence of your own with the word *sensitive*.**

_____

_____

**Instructor's Notes:** Read the explanatory paragraphs with the students. Then discuss the dictionary entry. Check students' knowledge of nouns, verbs, and adjectives. Read each set of directions with students.

61

## BACK TO THE STORY

**Remember:** What has happened in the story so far?

**Predict:** Look at the picture. What do you think will happen in the rest of the story?

# Amazing Mary

At the new school, Mary's life changed. One woman who worked there was a sensitive person. She saw that Mary was smart and guessed that Mary had *dyslexia* (dis **lek´** see uh). Dyslexia is a learning disability that makes reading and writing difficult. The school sent Mary to Upward Bound, a special summer program at the University of Oregon.

For the first time, Mary didn't have to conceal her learning disability. Two teachers who knew how to assist her worked with

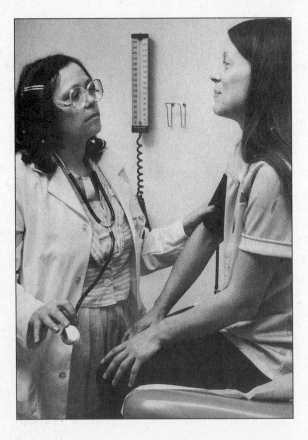

Mary. They instructed her in reading, writing, and arithmetic all day. Mary didn't resent the hard work. She was overcome with joy. "They were wonderful to me; they told me I was intelligent. They taught me how to deal with my dyslexia, how to read and write. They turned on my mind to the joy of learning." The teachers also taught Mary how to deal with her anger. "Use it to push your ambition," they told her.

That summer Mary's reading level went from first grade to eighth grade, with an A average. Within a year she had earned her G.E.D. certificate. Mary began to enjoy living as never before. "Upward Bound touched something deep inside me," Mary said, "a thrill of learning and enjoyment of living I had never experienced before." Never again would she endure the unbearable pain of feeling worthless.

**Instructor's Notes:** Read the questions with students. Help students review and predict. Locate the phonetic respelling of *dyslexia* and explain that the syllables in parentheses are there to help sound out this word. Then have students read the story silently.

Mary went home to visit her parents when she was seventeen. For the first time she talked to them about her future. "I want to be a doctor," she told them. Mary felt that her life had been different from the life of most doctors. She believed she could bring something special to the role of a physician.

"I always thought of this as a dream," Mary said. "When I was growing up, men were doctors and women were nurses." But Mary was determined to live her dream. She would be a doctor. Her dedication to this goal would carry her through many hard times.

## Disaster Strikes

Mary might never have dared to dream of being a doctor if she had seen the future. Before she could get very far in college, Mary had two children. She almost died giving birth to the second baby. Her heart stopped five times. She had a severe stroke, a loss of blood to the brain. Then Mary was in bed for months, and she lost almost half of her body weight. She couldn't control her muscles. Even worse, all of her learning had disappeared. She couldn't read, write, or even speak a single word. Life became a horrible nightmare.

Mary's father worked with her every night. He moved her hands in circles over and over again until Mary could draw the circles herself. Slowly she learned to walk, read, and write again.

As Mary struggled, she concentrated on her ambition. She *was* going to get out of that bed. She *was* going to read and write again. And she *was* going to become a physician.

## On Her Way

Mary finally enrolled in college again. But she was not a normal college student. She worked from 4 A.M. until noon, went to school in the afternoon, and played with her children in the evening. Then she studied for a few hours. After getting five or six hours of sleep, she started all over again.

The unbearable workload discouraged Mary. "You're crazy if you think you're going to be a doctor," she told herself. She thought about killing herself. But Mary Groda had a fire inside of her that wouldn't go out. "You're not going to cop out," she thought. "You're going to work and study harder. And you're going to make it."

Once again her dedication to her goal of becoming a doctor pulled her through.

Mary still had trouble making her muscles work right, so she decided to take a karate class. There she met David Lewis, a quiet, sensitive Vietnam veteran. In 1978 they got married. They moved to White Plains, New York, where David had a job as a newspaper reporter. Mary Groda-Lewis took classes at a local college. She graduated in 1980, 11 years after first enrolling in college. She was almost thirty-one years old.

## Doctor Mary

In her last year in college, Mary wrote to 15 medical schools. She asked them to take her as a student. But every one of the schools turned her down.

Mary could have been overcome by this severe setback, but her will to succeed was strong. The next year she decided to write to all the schools again and tell them the story of her life. This time seven schools agreed to talk to her. She went to Albany Medical College for an interview. "I was sort of bowled over from the beginning," said the man who interviewed Mary. "This was someone who needed a shot."

Albany Medical College accepted her as a student in 1980. Mary cried tears of joy. Her dream was not dead.

Nine months later, Mary cried again. The competition among students scared her. Despite Mary's hard work, her reading problems came back, and David had to read her assignments to her. Once again she had to conceal her disability. She was afraid that a teacher would tell her, "There's been a mistake. You don't belong here." When the first year ended, Mary had failed three courses. She was ready to quit.

Friends wouldn't let Mary quit. "School is tough," they said, "but so are you." Mary enrolled in summer school. In three months she made up the work, and then no one could stop her.

Mary's real talent was with patients. Although people knew that she was only a student, they felt that she cared about them. They trusted her and asked for "Doctor Mary."

## Popular Mary

In May of 1984 Mary's dream came true at last. She was thirty-five, the oldest woman in her class, and she graduated from medical school. She even won four awards for her dedication and her sensitive approach to patients.

The next stop in Mary's career took her to Youngstown, Ohio. For three years she worked in a hospital there. Her patients and co-workers observed the same dedication that had won her those awards. The head of the hospital called Mary "one of the very best." Others commented on her willingness to assist anyone, no matter what needed to be done. A nurse told Mary, "You're the first doctor who made up a bed or mopped up a mess on the floor. And you never made us feel that you were doing us a favor." Other doctors didn't resent the fact that Mary was so popular. One doctor predicted, "She's going to be a physician to whom people will flock."

Mary had borrowed money to go to medical school. "I am $50,000 in debt," she said after she began her practice. She had 20 years to pay back the loans, which were guaranteed by the government. To get the money, Mary agreed to work for four years in a part of the country that needs doctors. She was sent to Buhl (byool), a small town near Twin Falls, Idaho, in 1987.

Doctor Mary works with people "from birth to death," as she puts it. Most of her patients are migrant farm workers. "Thank God there are no strawberries here," she says with a laugh. She and one other doctor take care of about 15,000 people who live in the area.

## Dr. Mary's Story

A TV movie about Mary Groda's life, starring Kristy McNichol, was made in 1985. Like everyone else who has ever met Mary, Kristy was impressed. "Her determination and courage amazed me," Kristy said. "With all that she went through, she never lost sight of her goal."

Doctor Mary says that the movie hasn't had much effect on her life. "It was exciting when it first came out," she said, "but I'm glad it's over."

Dr. Mary Groda-Lewis offers some advice that she hopes will assist other adults who are trying to get an education and improve their lives. "I think the greatest gift you can give yourself is honesty and perseverance," she said. "I couldn't bear to think of the many years it would take to become a doctor, so I set smaller goals. I'd say, 'If I can make these next two years, I'll make it.' Sometimes it was, 'If I pass this test, I'll be OK.' I think you can do a lot of damage if you set your goals too far in advance."

Mary has one other bit of advice. "One of the hardest lessons in life is to learn to like yourself," she once said. "It took me a long time to learn to love being me."

Sometimes the simplest lessons are the hardest to learn.

# Comprehension

## Think About It

1. What learning disability kept Mary from doing well in school when she was young?
2. What other obstacles did Mary overcome to achieve her dream of becoming a doctor?
3. How did Mary get into medical school?
4. Sum up what happened in the story.

## Write About It

Reread the last three paragraphs of the story. What do you think of the advice Mary Groda-Lewis gives to adult learners?

**Instructor's Notes:** Have students read and answer the questions. **Write About It** can be used as a writing or discussion assignment.

# Comprehension: Recalling Facts/Main Idea

**A. Answer each question using a complete sentence.**

1. Who taught Mary to read? _____

   _____

2. What is dyslexia? _____

   _____

3. When did Mary graduate from college? _____

   _____

4. How did Mary deal with her reading problems in medical

   school? _____

   _____

5. Why did Mary want to become a doctor? _____

   _____

   _____

6. Where did Mary meet David? _____

   _____

7. Why doesn't Mary like strawberries?_____

   _____

**B. Choose the sentence that best states the main idea. Fill in the circle.**

The main idea of the whole story is

○ **a.** Anyone who goes to college can become a doctor.

○ **b.** With hard work and determination, you can reach your goals.

○ **c.** People who work hard at karate can go to college.

**Instructor's Notes:** Read the directions with students. For A, point out the first word in each question. These words are clues that help readers recall facts. For B, remind students that recalling the main idea means finding a statement that summarizes the story.

# Comprehension: Sequence

**Sequence** is about time. It means the 1-2-3 order in which things happen. Some key words can act as **sequence signs** in a story. Look for these words as you read. They will help you understand the order of events in a story. Here are some important sequence signs.

- Time words such as *tomorrow, yesterday, last week, in the morning*
- Days of the week and months of the year
- Dates such as *May of 1984*
- Times such as *noon, 4 A.M.*
- Words that tie two or more events together such as *before, when, after, while, during, next, finally*
- The ending *-ed* on verbs such as *assisted* and *concealed*. These endings tell you the action happened in the past.

**Read the paragraph below to find the sequence in which things happened. Fill in the circle for the words that best complete the sentence.**

Mary Groda was born in San Antonio, Texas, in 1949. She was the second of seven children. Her father lost his business in 1953. Her mother worked as a nurse, but the large family had trouble paying its bills. When Mary was six years old, the family became farm workers. They picked crops in farms across Texas and then Oregon. After the house they built near Portland was destroyed in a storm, the Groda family moved to the city.

Mary's family became farm workers

○ 1. when they moved to Portland.
○ 2. before Mary was born.
○ 3. after her father lost his business.

**Answer:** Choice 3. Choice 1 is wrong because the Grodas moved to Portland *after* they became farm workers. Choice 2 is wrong because Mary was born *before* the family became farm workers.

**Instructor's Notes:** Discuss the sequence signs with students. Read together the directions for the exercise and discuss the answers and explanation. Have the students write a paragraph containing sequence signs in their journals.

# Comprehension: Sequence

**A. Write *1, 2, 3,* and *4* to show the order in which things happened in the story.**

_____ Mary earned her G.E.D. certificate.

_____ Mary graduated from medical school.

_____ David and Mary got married.

_____ Mary was sent to reform school.

**B. Fill in the circle for the words that best complete each sentence.**

1. Mary learned to read

   ○ **a.** during the summer she spent in Upward Bound.
   ○ **b.** before she went to reform school.
   ○ **c.** after she left reform school and returned to Portland.

2. David and Mary met

   ○ **a.** before Mary went to reform school.
   ○ **b.** while Mary was in Upward Bound.
   ○ **c.** after Mary had a stroke.

3. Albany Medical College agreed to interview Mary

   ○ **a.** the first time she asked them.
   ○ **b.** after she wrote the second time and told her life story.
   ○ **c.** when she was in her last year of college.

4. Mary graduated from medical school

   ○ **a.** in 1978.
   ○ **b.** in 1980.
   ○ **c.** in 1984.

5. Mary worked in a hospital in Youngstown, Ohio

   ○ **a.** before she went to Buhl, Idaho.
   ○ **b.** after she went to Buhl, Idaho.
   ○ **c.** in 1985.

Sometimes people write so quickly that they leave out an important part of the sentence. A group of words that begins with a capital letter and ends with a punctuation mark isn't always a sentence.

**Example:** Graduated from medical school in 1984.
To make this group of words part of a sentence, add a subject. Tell *who* or *what*.
Mary Groda graduated from medical school in 1984.

**Example:** The children in school.
To make this group of words part of a sentence, add a predicate. Tell *what* was done.
The children in school made fun of Mary's clothes.

**A. Each sentence below is a fragment. Fill in the circle beside the part of the sentence that is missing.**

1. The Groda family.
   ○ **a.** subject       ○ **b.** predicate

2. Couldn't control her muscles.
   ○ **a.** subject       ○ **b.** predicate

3. Accepted Mary as a student.
   ○ **a.** subject       ○ **b.** predicate

4. The doctors who worked with Mary.
   ○ **a.** subject       ○ **b.** predicate

**B. Change each of the fragments above to make a complete sentence. Begin with a capital letter and end with a period.**

1. _____

2. _____

3. _____

4. _____

**Instructor's Notes:** Discuss the definition of a complete sentence with students and explain that an incomplete sentence is a fragment. Some students may need additional work with the concept of subject and predicate. Read each set of directions with students.

# Life Skill: Completing a Medical Form

When you go to a doctor or clinic, you are asked to fill out a medical form. This form asks for facts such as your name, address, and date of birth. It also asks about your health and medical history. It is important to fill out a medical form as accurately as you can. That way the doctors and nurses who read it know what your medical history is.

Read the medical form below. The first part asks for information about you. The second part asks about diseases and some common health problems. The last questions ask about other important things a doctor should know.

**Fill out the medical form.**

---

## MEDICAL HISTORY FORM

**PERSONAL INFORMATION**

Date _____   Social Security # _____   Date of birth _____   Age _____

Name _____   Sex: M _____  F _____   Place of birth _____

Current address _____City _____   State ____ Zip _____

Phone number:  work _____   home _____

Marital status:   single _____   married _____   divorced _____   Number of children _____   Ages _____

**PERSONAL MEDICAL HISTORY**

1. Check (√) if you have ever had:

____ allergies          ____ chicken pox          ____ German measles (rubella)     ____ measles
____ appendicitis       ____ diabetes             ____ heart disease                ____ mumps
____ arthritis          ____ dizziness            ____ hepatitis                    ____ pneumonia
____ asthma             ____ epilepsy             ____ kidney stones                ____ ulcers
____ bronchitis

2. Have you had major surgery?  yes _____  no _____   For what? _____   When? _____

3. Are you taking any medications now?  yes _____  no _____   List your medications here. _____

4. Are you allergic to any medicines?  Please list. _____

5. Do you have any other allergies ? Please list. _____

**FAMILY MEDICAL HISTORY**

List blood relatives (mother, father, sisters, brothers, or grandparents) who have had:

____ high blood pressure     ____ tuberculosis      ____ heart disease      ____ sickle cell anemia
____ stroke                  ____ epilepsy          ____ diabetes
____ other _____

---

# *Charge It!*

Buy Now,
Pay Later!

## DISCUSSION

### Remember

Look at the picture. Have you ever been in an appliance store like this?

### Predict

Look at the picture and the story title. What do you think this story is about?

**Instructor's Notes:** Read the discussion questions with students. Discuss the story title, the characters, and the situation in the photo.

"Folks, I can fix you up with one of these for just a little bit down and a little bit a month," the salesclerk said. Fred and Anita Johnson lingered in front of the washing machine. They really needed one now that they had a new baby. Fred didn't like going out to wash clothes after he got home from work. Anita went to school every day and had to study most evenings. Having a washing machine at home would make their lives much easier.

Fred and Anita looked at each other. "Can we afford it?" Fred asked Anita.

"You can't afford not to have it!" the salesclerk said.

"I don't know," Anita replied to Fred, as she pulled him aside so the salesclerk couldn't hear. The salesclerk smiled at Anita over Fred's shoulder and held her order book. The words *Buy Now, Pay Later* leaped at Fred from a sign on the wall.

"We only have to pay $20 now and $20 a month," Fred said.

"Yes, but we'll have to keep on paying $20 a month for two years," Anita said. "I'm not sure I want to borrow that much money right now. We can really use the washer, but I just don't feel good about buying on credit."

"Well, the important thing is that we get the washer now. We need it for the baby," Fred said. "We just paid off the car. Let's do it."

"OK," Anita said. The salesclerk was now standing near them in front of a clothes dryer.

"We'll have you washing in no time," the clerk said. "Now, have you thought about how you're going to dry all those wet clothes in your apartment?"

**Instructor's Notes:** Have students read the next two pages silently, circling words they don't recognize. Review the circled words. Discuss the meaning of the phrase *read the fine print*: "make sure you understand the details and rules."

### Buy Now and Pay Later!

Buy now and pay later is what credit is all about. Credit allows you to buy things you need even though you don't have the money to pay for them right now. Buying everything from cars to clothes on credit has become a popular way of life in America.

"Incredible!" you say. "Where do I sign up?" Slow down. Think first. Remember that credit isn't an invitation to rush out and buy everything you always wanted. Credit carries certain duties with it. Before you get yourself into debt, let's *read the fine print* and see how credit really works.

When you use credit, you borrow money. You guarantee that you will pay it back. The person you borrow from is really saying that he or she trusts you.

"Fine," you say. "*Now* can I sign up?" Wait a minute. First, think about how the person lending the money looks at the situation. People who lend money, lenders, don't want to give credit to just anyone. They want to be sure they lend money only to people who are likely to pay it back on time. They only want to lend money to people who will be a good credit risk.

How can someone know that you are a good credit risk? If you have borrowed money before and have paid it back on time, you've shown that you are a good credit risk. If you haven't borrowed before, lenders will have to question you in great detail. Here are some of the questions they will ask you when they check your credit.

- Do you have a steady job? Have you worked at the same place for some time?
- Have you lived at the same address for a long time?
- Do you have a savings account? Could you start one and add to it each month?
- Have you ever bought a car, clothes, or household items *on time*?

If you answered *yes* to most of the questions above, you may not be far away from the day when you can say, "Charge it, please!"

# Vocabulary: Definitions

**Read each paragraph below. Notice how the other words in each sentence help define the new word. Match the vocabulary words with their meanings. Write the letter.**

accurate
apply
establish
financial
installment

The only way to **establish** a credit history is to borrow money. Jane and Howard Morgan have never had a loan before, but they decided to **apply** for credit to buy a TV. They met with the store's credit manager, who wanted to get an **accurate** picture of the Morgans' **financial** situation. Could they afford to pay the **installment** each month?

_____ 1. establish     **a.** make a request; ask

_____ 2. apply     **b.** having to do with money

_____ 3. accurate     **c.** set up or make firm

_____ 4. financial     **d.** part of a debt to be paid at a stated time

_____ 5. installment     **e.** correct

notify
obligation
previous
qualify
reference

The credit manager has to predict whether the Morgans will meet this **obligation**. She asks the Morgans to fill out a form to determine if they **qualify** for credit. The form asks them to list their current and **previous** employers. The form also asks for the name and address of a personal **reference**. After the credit manager contacts the Morgans' bank and reference, she will **notify** the Morgans of her decision.

_____ 6. obligation     **f.** coming before; earlier

_____ 7. qualify     **g.** let know; inform

_____ 8. previous     **h.** meet necessary conditions

_____ 9. reference     **i.** duty based on a promise or contract

_____ 10. notify     **j.** someone who can give information about you

**75**

**Instructor's Notes:** Read the directions and the new sight words with students. Explain that the directions apply to both sets of words and paragraphs. Point out that the characters in these two paragraphs are new characters that did not appear in the story opener. When students complete the exercises, discuss the clues that helped students match the words and definitions.

# Vocabulary: Suffixes

A **suffix** is a word part added to the end of a word to change the word's function and meaning. Adding a suffix usually changes the part of speech of the word.

The suffixes –*er* and –*or* both mean *one who*. When you add –*er* or –*or* to a verb, you change it to a noun that tells who or what performs the action. For example, –*er* added to *employ* becomes *employer*, or someone who hires others to work.

creditor     borrower     counselor     consumer

**The words in color have the suffix –*er* or –*or*. Read the sentences below. Then rewrite each sentence, using one of the words in color to replace the underlined words.**

1. Carol talked to a <u>person who gives advice</u> in the financial aid office.

   _____

   _____

2. She wanted to consider all the choices before becoming <u>a person who takes money as a loan</u>.

   _____

   _____

3. Carol's parents taught her to be a wise <u>person who uses goods or services</u>.

   _____

   _____

4. She knows about buying on credit and understands her obligation to the <u>person to whom the money is due</u>.

   _____

   _____

**Instructor's Notes:** Review the definition of *suffix* with students. Examine the words in color, noting which end in -*er* and which in -*or*. Read the directions with students.

# Word Study: Prefixes and Suffixes

A **prefix** is a word part that comes before the base word:
<u>pre</u>heat    <u>re</u>act    <u>un</u>lace    <u>de</u>frost

A **suffix** is a word part that comes after the base word:
thought<u>less</u>    cheer<u>ful</u>    kind<u>ness</u>    pay<u>ment</u>

**Tips for Dividing Words with Prefixes and Suffixes**

- When the base word has only one syllable, it's easy to divide the word. **Examples: un**/lace, kind/**ness**

- Some base words have more than one syllable. With these words, find the prefix or suffix first. Then use the vowel patterns you've learned to divide the rest of the word into syllables. **Examples: un**/wel/come, **re**/ad/mit, es/tab/lish/**ment**

- Some words may have a prefix <u>and</u> a suffix, or more than one suffix. Use the patterns you've learned to divide the words into syllables. **Examples:** cheer/**ful**/**ness**, **un**/help/**ful**, **re**/en/list/**ment**

**Divide the words in color into syllables. Then read the sentence and circle the meaning of the word as it is used in the sentence.**

1. The bill is **payable** as soon as you receive it. _____

   due    late    filed

2. He got a letter about **nonpayment** of his telephone bill.

   _____

   right to ignore    failure to pay    ability to understand

3. She was **uncomfortable** about the price of the washing

   machine. _____

   pleased    angry    worried

**Instructor's Notes:** Discuss the explanation and tips with students. Read the directions and have students complete the exercise independently. Ask students to add prefixes and suffixes to some of the new words in this unit (Ex: *inaccurate*).

## BACK TO THE STORY

**Remember:** What have you learned so far about Fred and Anita's needs and their concerns about obtaining credit?

**Predict:** Look at the picture. What do you think is happening?

# Charge It!

Before you apply for credit, you need to know about credit charges, credit records, and your rights under the law. You also need to know where to get help if you can't pay your debts.

Let's get back to Fred and Anita Johnson who have applied for credit to buy the washing machine. Fred has a steady job. The Johnsons have $500 in their savings account. This month they made the last payment on their car. They list as references their landlord, Fred's employer, and the bank that loaned them the money to buy their car. The store's credit manager will talk to these people to decide if the Johnsons are a good credit risk.

If the Johnsons qualify for credit, the store will charge a fee called *interest* or a *finance charge*. The price of that new washer might be $400, but only if the Johnsons paid cash right now. If they buy it on the installment plan, they will pay a finance charge of about $1\frac{1}{2}$ percent per month on the unpaid balance. If the Johnsons pay for the washer in 24 installments, the washer will cost them $479.04.

To be a smart consumer, know exactly what you're getting into. Read the credit application carefully. It states the interest rate the store charges and the terms for payment. If you have any questions, talk to the credit manager. Make sure you understand the contract before you sign it. Not all stores and banks charge the same

**Instructor's Notes:** Read the questions with students. Help students review and predict. Then have students read the story silently. Explain that a *credit bureau* is a separate organization from the store or bank that loaned the money.

interest rate, so shop around. Look at the *total* cost of the item including finance charges. The lowest total cost is your best deal.

### Keeping Your Record Clean

When you buy on credit, you promise to pay back the money you borrowed to make your purchase. If you don't repay the money, the creditor can take back the goods you bought. So if the Johnsons buy the washer on credit and don't meet their payments, the store can take back the washing machine. The Johnsons will lose the washer and the money they've paid toward it. They will also establish a bad credit record.

How you handle your debts becomes part of your credit history. A good credit record tells lenders that they can trust you. Many creditors send information on how you pay your debts to a credit bureau. A credit bureau keeps a file on you that shows how well you've met your financial obligations. Your credit record reveals whether you've made payments on time or you've failed to repay a loan.

When you apply for credit, the lender will call a credit bureau for information on how you have paid installment debts in the past. Late payments and unpaid debts can ruin your credit record. Remember these tips.

- Make all monthly installments on time. All late payments as well as unpaid debts are listed on your credit record.
- Don't overuse your credit. If you are spending more than 15 percent of your income on credit payments (not counting house and car payments), you have borrowed too much money.

Lenders use credit bureaus to protect themselves from people who are poor credit risks. By investigating your credit history, a lender can predict whether you'll repay a new loan. Creditors would go out of business if no one paid them back. They can take the matter to court when people don't make their payments.

### Your Credit Rights

The law protects creditors from people who don't repay their loans. The law also protects you, as a user of credit. For example, you have a right to see the contents of your credit record.

Credit bureaus don't make up the information in your record. They collect information from your creditors. Lenders use that information to decide whether you can borrow money. So you want the information in your credit record to be accurate.

Your community may have more than one credit bureau. To find out which one has your records, call your creditors. Ask which credit bureau they use. Or ask your bank for the names and addresses of credit bureaus in your area.

Most credit bureaus will give you a copy of your record for about $10. If a lender has refused to give you credit, you can get a copy of your record for free. Some people pay to check their credit record before they need to qualify for a loan. They want to make sure the information in their file is accurate before they apply.

### Checking Your Credit Record

To get a copy of your credit record, follow these steps.

1. Write to the credit bureau and ask for a copy of your credit record. Include the following information:
   - your full legal name;
   - other legal names you've used in the past (for example, a woman's name before she married);
   - your current address;
   - previous addresses, if you've been at your present address less than five years;
   - your Social Security number; and
   - your driver's license number.

2. Include a check or money order for the cost of the copy. If you are asking for a free copy because a lender turned you down, send a copy of the lender's letter.

3. Keep a copy of your letter. If you don't receive your report in ten days, send another copy of your letter to the credit bureau. Write NOT RECEIVED in red ink across the top.

Read your credit report carefully. If it isn't accurate, notify the credit bureau right away. You are responsible for proving to the credit bureau that the information is not correct. For example, if your report states that you did not repay a loan that you have paid off, call the lender. Ask the lender to send a letter to the credit bureau stating that the loan has been repaid. Also send your request in writing.

The law states that the credit bureau must investigate your record and correct any mistakes within 45 days. Check by phone and mail to be sure the changes have been made.

## What If You Really Are in Trouble?

Let's hope that your credit record is in good shape, but what if it isn't? What if it contains information that is not favorable but true?

Ten years ago, after Fred Johnson enlisted in the military, he had trouble meeting his credit obligations. His father was in the hospital with a severe injury, and Fred faced huge hospital and doctor bills. Fortunately, Fred didn't try to conceal the problem. He notified his creditors right away. He told them why he was having financial problems. The creditors understood Fred's situation. They were willing to let Fred adapt his payment plan so he could meet his obligations. Because Fred didn't wait until he was months behind in his payments, the lenders believed his story.

## Where To Go for Help

Fred got in touch with a debt counselor to get professional help with his problem. The counselor informed Fred of his credit rights. Together they cleaned up his bad credit record.

The law allowed Fred to add a short statement to his credit record to explain why he got behind in his payments. He had this statement sent to anyone who asked for his credit record. His debt counselor helped him write the statement for his record.

The debt counselor assisted Fred in other ways, too. Lenders had called Fred at home and work asking for the money that he owed. They had threatened to take part of his wages. However, they stopped calling once they learned that Fred was working with a debt counselor.

Fred's debt counselor also gave him good advice. The counselor told Fred to stop using credit and asked him to cut up his credit cards. Then the counselor showed Fred how to manage his money better and put him on a plan to make his payments on time. With the counselor's help, Fred eventually paid off his debts. By the time he married Anita, he had overcome his financial problems.

## And Now for the Good News

Fred's past problems won't hurt the Johnsons' chances of getting that washer. The Johnsons got a car loan two years ago, despite Fred's previous credit history. They've paid off the car, which is further evidence that they are now a good credit risk. They no longer have to worry about their credit references, but they do need to consider how they're going to buy that clothes dryer.

Like Fred Johnson, most people have money problems at some time. Often these problems can be solved. You may be able to pay off your debts, or you might get a job that pays more money. Lenders know that just because you once had problems, you aren't always going to be a bad credit risk.

Many creditors are interested in your credit record for the last three to five years. By law, information about late payments stays on your credit record for only seven years after you settle the debt. After seven years, your bad record is wiped out if you have no new problems. Even if you have had money problems in the past, you can still establish a good credit record in the future.

The best way to protect your credit record is to use credit carefully. Don't borrow more than you can afford to pay back. Think before you say "charge it," and always read the fine print!

# Comprehension

### Think About It

1. What is an advantage of buying on credit? A disadvantage?
2. How can you find out about your own credit record?
3. Sum up some important points about credit.

### Write About It

What are your experiences buying on credit? What advice would you give to others based on your experience?

**Instructor's Notes:** Have students read and answer the questions. **Write About It** can be used as a writing or discussion assignment.

# Comprehension: Recalling Facts/Cause and Effect

**A. Answer these questions using complete sentences.**

1. Who can give you professional help with debt problems?

   _____

2. What can ruin your credit record? _____

   _____

3. Where can you get a record of how well your creditors say

   you've paid your debts? _____

   _____

4. When should you contact a debt counselor? _____

   _____

   _____

5. Why do you pay more when you buy something on credit?

   _____

6. If you have had problems paying your debts in the past, how
   long will that information remain in your credit record?

   _____

   _____

**B. Study each sentence. Are the words in color the *cause* or the
*effect*? Fill in the circle beside the correct answer.**

1. Ten years ago, Fred Johnson had trouble paying his debts
   because he had to pay his father's hospital and doctor bills

   ○ cause      ○ effect

2. Fred's creditors were willing to adapt his payment plan so
   he could meet his obligations

   ○ cause      ○ effect

---

**Instructor's Notes:** Read the directions with students. For A, remind students that the words that begin
each question call for facts. For B, review the definitions of *cause* and *effect*.

# Comprehension: Drawing Conclusions

A **conclusion** is an opinion or judgment you make after studying all the facts you have. The conclusion is usually not stated directly in what you read. You draw a conclusion based on what you know and what you have learned by reading. You have to *read between the lines* to draw a conclusion.

> **How To Draw a Conclusion:**
>
> 1. Read the paragraph or story.
> 2. Recall or list all the facts.
> 3. Think about the facts. Then *read between the lines.*
> 4. Draw a conclusion. (Check yourself by asking if the facts support your conclusion.)

**A. Read this paragraph about credit.**

Richard got a raise at his job. He bought a new car and TV on credit. He also moved to a bigger house. Now Richard is having trouble paying his monthly bills.

**B. List the facts.**

Fact 1: _____

Fact 2: _____

Fact 3: _____

Fact 4: _____

**C. Which is the best conclusion to draw?**

○ 1. Richard works many overtime hours at his job.
○ 2. Richard pays his bills on time.
○ 3. Richard used credit to buy more than he could afford.

**Answer:** Choice 3. Choice 2 is wrong because the facts in the paragraph say just the opposite. Choice 1 is wrong because the facts don't support it.

**Instructor's Notes:** Discuss the tips with students. Read together the directions for the exercises and discuss the answers and explanation in C. Have students write a paragraph that states a conclusion in their journals.

# Comprehension: Drawing Conclusions

**A. Read each statement below. Fill in the circle beside the best answer.**

1. Reread paragraph 2 on page 78. What conclusion can you draw?

   ○ **a.** You can get credit anywhere by just asking for it.
   ○ **b.** You must have a certain financial background to get credit.
   ○ **c.** Anyone who wants credit must have a new car.

2. Reread paragraph 4 on page 78. What conclusion can you draw?

   ○ **a.** Creditors cheat consumers by charging them interest.
   ○ **b.** The Johnsons can save money by paying finance charges.
   ○ **c.** The Johnsons should buy the washer *on time* only if they can afford the price plus the finance charges.

3. Reread the section "Your Credit Rights." What conclusion can you draw?

   ○ **a.** Accurate credit records are important for borrowers and lenders.
   ○ **b.** Credit bureaus make up the information in your credit records.
   ○ **c.** You can get a copy of your credit record for $50.

**B. Read each question and write your conclusion.**

1. After reading the story, do you think the Johnsons will buy the clothes dryer on credit? Tell why you think this.

   _____

   _____

2. Suppose the Johnsons had trouble making their monthly installments on the car they bought two years ago. Would they get credit to buy that washing machine now?

   _____

   _____

**Instructor's Notes:** Read each set of directions with students. Review the steps to drawing a conclusion on page 84.

Verbs show what happened and the time of the action. **Past tense verbs** tell whether an action took place in the immediate past (the past tense) or the more distant past (the past participle). Form the past and past participle of regular verbs by adding –*ed* to the present tense. The past participle also takes a helping verb (have, has, or had).

> **Present:** I want a good credit rating.
> **Past:** Yesterday I wanted to buy a tape recorder.
> **Past Participle:** I had wanted to pay for it in installments.

**A.** **Form the past participle of some irregular verbs by adding a helping verb to the past tense, as in the example below. Fill in each blank with the correct past participle.**

| Present | Past | Past Participle | |
|---------|------|-----------------|---|
| 1. keep | kept | have, has, had | kept |
| 2. fight | fought | have, has, had | |
| 3. bring | brought | have, has, had | |
| 4. stand | stood | have, has, had | |

**B.** **For many irregular verbs the present tense, the past tense, and the past participle are all different words. Read the verbs below. Then write the correct verbs in the sentences.**

| Present | Past | Past Participle |
|---------|------|-----------------|
| see | saw | have, has, had seen |
| forget | forgot | have, has, had forgotten |
| throw | threw | have, has, had thrown |
| give | gave | have, has, had given |

(see)    1. I _____ an overdue notice in the mail yesterday.

(throw)    2. I guess I _____ away the bill by mistake.

(give)    3. My creditor has _____ me ten days to pay.

**Instructor's Notes:** Review the definitions of *verb* and *past tense* with students. Then read each set of directions. Some students may need additional practice using irregular past tense verbs correctly.

# Life Skill: Filling Out a Credit Application

To buy something on credit, you must first fill out a credit application. Fill out the form accurately and completely. Before you apply for credit, gather addresses (including ZIP codes) and phone numbers for your place of employment, personal references, and banks; your bank account and charge account numbers; and your Social Security or alien I.D. number.

Read and fill out the credit application below. Read the sentence that appears above the space for your signature carefully. When you sign the form, you give the store the right to check your references and report your credit record to the credit bureau.

## Credit Account Application

**Please indicate below name in which account is to be carried. Applicant, if married, may apply for a separate account.**

| ☐ Mr.   ☐ Miss<br>☐ Mrs.   ☐ Ms. | First Name | | Initial | | Last Name | | |
|---|---|---|---|---|---|---|---|

| Address (to which you want your billing mailed) | | Apt. # | City | | State | | Zip Code |
|---|---|---|---|---|---|---|---|
| Home Address | | Apt. # | City | | State | | Zip Code |

| Home Phone | | Business Phone | Social Security Number | | Age | Number of Dependents (excluding Applicant) | |
|---|---|---|---|---|---|---|---|

| Are you a United States Citizen? ☐ Yes ☐ No | If no, state immigration status | | | | Are you a permanent resident? | ☐ Yes ☐ No | |
|---|---|---|---|---|---|---|---|

| How long at present address? Yrs. Mos. | ☐ Own   ☐ Rent   ☐ Board   ☐ Live with parents | | | | Monthly rent or Mortgage Payments $ | | |
|---|---|---|---|---|---|---|---|

| Name of Landlord or Mortgage Holder | | Street Address | City | | State | | Zip Code |
|---|---|---|---|---|---|---|---|

| Previous Address (if less than 2 years at present address) | | | | | How Long? Yrs. Mos. | | |
|---|---|---|---|---|---|---|---|

| Employer | | Street Address | City | | State | | Zip Code |
|---|---|---|---|---|---|---|---|

| How Long? Yrs. Mos. | Occupation | | | | Net Income (Take Home Pay) $ | ☐ Monthly ☐ Weekly | |
|---|---|---|---|---|---|---|---|

| Previous Employer (if less than one year with present employer) | | | | | How Long? Yrs. Mos. | | |
|---|---|---|---|---|---|---|---|

| Other income (if any) Amount $   ☐ Monthly ☐ Weekly | Source of Other Income | | NOTE: Alimony, child support or separate maintenance income need not be revealed if you do not wish to have it considered as a basis for paying this obligation. | | | | |
|---|---|---|---|---|---|---|---|

| Name and Address of Bank | | | | | ☐ Savings #<br>☐ Checking # | | |
|---|---|---|---|---|---|---|---|

| Relative or Personal Reference not living at above address | | Street Address | City | | State | | Zip Code |
|---|---|---|---|---|---|---|---|

| **CREDIT REFERENCES** | Charge Account, Loan References Store/Company Address | Date Opened | Name Account Carried In | Account Number | Balance | Monthly Payment |
|---|---|---|---|---|---|---|
| | | | | | | |
| | | | | | | |

If others are authorized to buy on the account print names here and state relationship:   1.          2.

This store is authorized to investigate my credit, employment, and income references, and to report my performance of the account to proper persons and bureaus.

**X** Signature of Applicant _____   Date _____

**Instructor's Notes:** Have students read the introduction silently. Then discuss the contents of the form before students fill it out. Use the Unit 5 Review on page 124 to conclude the unit. Then assign *Reading For Today Workbook Six*, Unit 5.

# A Problem in the Workplace

The term *sexual harassment* is often in the news. In your workplace, you've probably discussed the subject. It's a subject with many angles. Some of the angles have to do with the law. Other angles have to do with people's basic feelings about the roles of women and men.

Just what is sexual harassment? What does it mean to you? If you're like most people, your answer is based on your personal point of view. Take a look at four work situations. After you read each story, tell whether you think it describes a sexual harassment situation.

1.  Doris worked with Gary for a long time. In general, they had a good working relationship. Doris admired Gary's enthusiasm for his work. Gary admired Doris's intelligence and energy. There was one thing that always bothered Doris, though. Gary often made remarks about her figure and her clothes. Although this annoyed Doris, she never told Gary. One day, however, when Gary said, "Mmmm! Great dress, Doris! Nice short skirt!" Doris blew up at him.

    "I can't stand it when you say things like that to me! she said. "I hate those kinds of remarks! They make me feel like a sex object. I feel like you're harassing me."

2.  Milt's supervisor, Clare, often made suggestive remarks to him and told him off-color jokes when they were alone. Milt did not respond. He did not want to get involved with his boss on a personal level. Then Clare started inviting Milt to come to her house for supper. Milt always turned her down. Finally one day Clare said, "Listen, Milt. I don't think you get the picture. If you're not willing to do me a favor now and then, you're not going to last long around here!"

**Instructor's Notes:** Have students read the next two pages silently. Have them underline words they don't recognize. Review the underlined words. Check students' recognition of the term *angles* to be sure that they understand its meaning in the story context and do not confuse it with *angels*.

89

3.    Ruth Ann was the only female employee in a machine shop. She was the bookkeeper. The machinists had decorated the office with pictures and signs that appealed to them. Many of these pictures were offensive to Ruth Ann. She felt uneasy being surrounded by them. But worse than that, as far as Ruth Ann was concerned, were the off-color jokes the men told within her range of hearing. It made Ruth Ann nervous, and she found she was not doing her best work because she was so uncomfortable in this work situation.

4.    Jack and Rita were co-workers. They dated for a while. Then Jack broke up with Rita. She was very hurt and handled it badly. Then, every day she leaned on Jack with pleas to start dating again. She would hang around his desk and interrupt his work. She often called him on the intercom. Sometimes she made threats, such as "If you won't see me again, I'll tell the boss you're bothering me."

In your opinion, which—if any—of the four situations above are examples of sexual harassment? Why do you think so? As you think about these four situations, you'll probably find that the meaning of sexual harassment is not very clear. That's exactly why it's a big issue in offices and courtrooms all over the country.

# Vocabulary: Definitions

Read each paragraph below. Notice how the other words in each sentence help define the new word. Match the vocabulary words with their meanings. Write the letter.

conditions
emotions
environment
hostile
offensive

No one wants to work in an unfriendly or **hostile environment**. Whether it be a building site or an office, these working **conditions** create unhappy workers. Certain kinds of behavior are **offensive** and upsetting to most people. Pay and safety aren't the only things that matter; feelings and **emotions** about a place of work count too.

| _____ | 1. conditions | **a.** disagreeable |
| _____ | 2. emotions | **b.** unfriendly |
| _____ | 3. environment | **c.** situations |
| _____ | 4. hostile | **d.** surroundings |
| _____ | 5. offensive | **e.** feelings |

constitute
harassment
promotion
representative
supervisor

A **representative** from a government office came to speak to the workers. He talked about **harassment** at work. He explained that being continually disturbed **constituted** harassment. He gave this example of sexual harassment: when a **supervisor** asks for certain favors as a condition of getting ahead. In other words, you won't get a **promotion** unless you do what your boss wants.

| _____ | 6. constitute | **f.** boss |
| _____ | 7. harassment | **g.** advancement in position |
| _____ | 8. promotion | **h.** someone who speaks for a group |
| _____ | 9. representative | **i.** make up or form |
| _____ | 10. supervisor | **j.** repeatedly bothering someone |

**Instructor's Notes:** Read aloud the instructions and the words in color. Have students read the paragraphs and complete the exercises. Then discuss the clues that helped them match the words and definitions.

# Vocabulary: Analogies

An **analogy** is a comparison. It shows that a relationship between one pair of words is similar to the relationship between another pair of words. Study the kinds of analogies below.

> **a.** *Legal* is to *lawful* as *hostile* is to *unfriendly*.
> (relationship: mean the same, synonyms)
>
> **b.** *Offensive* is to *pleasing* as *gorgeous* is to *ugly*.
> (relationship: opposites, antonyms)
>
> **c.** *Minute* is to *hour* as *day* is to *week*.
> (relationship: a part to the whole)
>
> **d.** *Judge* is to *court* as *umpire* is to *baseball*.
> (relationship: use or function)

**Read the word pairs below. Decide how the first two words are related. Write the word to complete each analogy. Be ready to tell why your answer is the best.**

1. *Supervisor* is to *office* as *captain* is to _____ .
   a. company      b. ship      c. school

2. *Down* is to *up* as *many* is to _____ .
   a. few      b. numerous      c. low

3. *Emotions* are to *feelings* as *wishes* are to _____ .
   a. facts      b. terms      c. dreams

4. *Fair* is to *unfair* as *tough* is to _____ .
   a. difficult      b. tiny      c. easy

5. *Page* is to *newspaper* as *drawer* is to _____ .
   a. headline      b. desk      c. storage

6. *Victims* are to *sufferers* as *employees* are to _____ .
   a. workers      b. bosses      c. employers

7. *Fails* is to *succeeds* as *laughs* is to _____ .
   a. giggles      b. cries      c. overcomes

# Word Study: Pronunciations

Sometimes you can read a word, but you aren't sure how to say it. A dictionary includes a **respelling** of each entry word. This respelling is in parentheses and shows how to pronounce the word. To use these respellings, you may need to check the **pronunciation key**. It shows you how to "read" the letters and special symbols used in the respellings.

**Pronunciation Key:** Each symbol has the same sound as the darker letters in the key word.

| | | | | | | | | | |
|---|---|---|---|---|---|---|---|---|---|
| ə | ago | au | loud | ō | cone | th | then | zh | vision |
| ər | learn | e | bell | ȯ | saw, all, | u | cut | ´ | accented |
| a | map | ē | sweet | | water | ü | pool | | syllable |
| ā | day | ər | germ | oi | boy | u̇ | book | | |
| ä | father | i | rip | ər | mirror | û | perch | | |
| är | car | ī | side | th | thin | ər | vulture | | |

**Use the pronunciation key to help you say each respelled word below. Then fill in the circle that matches each respelling. Write the key word that tells you how to pronounce the symbol in color. The first one is done for you.**

1. (thrō) ○ through ● throw ○ threw ___cone___

2. (sək sēd´) ○ secure ○ scenery ○ succeed _____

3. (trüth) ○ truth ○ trust ○ turn _____

4. (pā´ shənt) ○ patent ○ potion ○ patient _____

5. (ish´ u̇) ○ island ○ issue ○ insult _____

6. (spoil) ○ spool ○ spoil ○ spot _____

7. (klau´ dē) ○ cloudy ○ clover ○ clever _____

8. (kə rekt´) ○ cork ○ correct ○ crack _____

9. (kül´ ər) ○ cooler ○ collar ○ color _____

10. (lē´ gəl) ○ ledge ○ legal ○ lady _____

**Instructor's Notes:** Review with students the pronunciation key and how to use it. Encourage students to refer to a dictionary for help when they read.

## BACK TO THE STORY

**Remember:** Why is sexual harassment a big issue today?

**Predict:** Read the subheads on this and the next two pages. What ideas do you think the rest of this article covers?

# A Problem in the Workplace

According to the law, there are two major kinds of sexual harassment. The legal terms may be new to you, but the situations they describe are familiar to many people in the workplace.

**I. Type I: *Quid Pro Quo* (Do It or Else!):** *Quid pro quo* is a Latin term meaning "something in return for something." In many workplaces it also unfortunately translates into "do sexual favors for your supervisor or lose your job." The victims are usually women. Thousands of women report being the victims of this kind of threat. Until recently, the decision women workers made often had to do with how badly they needed their jobs. However, women are learning to be more outspoken about their rights. Publicity on the topic of sexual harassment has helped. According to the law, no one has to put up with this kind of behavior or work environment. As more people become aware of this it becomes easier for them to speak out against harassment.

*Some companies hold regular sessions at which employees can discuss the company's rules.*

**Instructor's Notes:** Have students read silently. Then discuss why publicity about an issue makes it easier for people to talk about that issue. Point out that some words such as *supporting* have more than one meaning; "paying for"; "holding up." Have students use the words in sentences of their own to show different meanings.

The courts are very clear about *quid pro quo* cases. A 1980 federal rule says if doing sexual favors is made a condition of one's employment, that constitutes sexual harassment. This rule also covers cases where an employee doesn't get a raise or promotion because of not giving in to a supervisor's sexual demands. In the long run, the courts hold the employer, or company, responsible for sexual harassment by any supervisors in the company. That's because, say the courts, supervisors are representatives of their employers.

**2. Type 2: A Hostile Work Environment:** A hostile work environment is a workplace where the employee suffers emotionally—so much so that she or he can't get the job done properly. State and federal courts have ruled that people have a right to work in an environment that is free of insults and threats. In many workplaces, women have had to put up with off-color jokes, touches, gestures, name-calling, and propositions. If this is the everyday environment, and an employee suffers from it, then it's a hostile environment. And, just as in *quid pro quo,* courts hold the employee, or company, responsible for what goes on in a workplace.

### Making a Complaint

It's up to the courts to decide whether a workplace is a hostile environment for an employee or whether a *quid pro quo* situation exists. And of course, the courts can't make that decision unless the employee brings the complaint into the courtroom.

Going to court with a complaint is a last resort though. An employee's first step is to file a complaint with his or her employer. This can be the beginning of a long, tough process. Some employers nowadays respond quickly to complaints about sexual harassment. But many businesses don't want to hear about it. Employers often say the employee is "imagining things" or has a grudge against a supervisor. And in many cases, there has been an honest misunderstanding between men and women about what's offensive and what's not.

### The Last Resort

What if an employee complains about harassment and the employer fails to correct the situation? If the employee wants to take the case into court, then she or he has to bring in some evidence. Evidence can be made up of:

- Careful notes about the time, place, and nature of each offensive event
- Witnesses who heard the *quid pro quo* propositions or saw and heard the offensive remarks.
- Witnesses who have had to suffer through the same propositions or put up with the same hostile work environment.

Without this kind of evidence, a court trial can just turn into an argument about who said what—for example, the supervisor can swear that the incident never took place; while the employee can swear that it did. In harassment cases, courts usually rule in favor of the employer, unless the employee brings in records or witnesses. However, if the employee does win in court, it can mean that the company will have to pay him or her for the pain of being harassed.

*This employee tells the personnel director about her complaint.*

## Interpreting the Law

You've read about what the law says on the issue of sexual harassment. Now think about the next cases.

1. George is a long-time employee at XYZ Industries. He's next in line for a promotion. Then Liz, a new supervisor, arrives. She says she won't give George the promotion unless he dates her. Some of George's friends have heard Liz make this proposal to him.

2. June says she constantly has to put up with her supervisor's *quid pro quo* proposals. According to June, the supervisor says he'll fire her unless she has a romantic relationship with him. The supervisor denies he ever made such proposals.

3. Loretta says she is so nervous in her office environment that she can't work well anymore. Some of the men in the office repeatedly make sexual remarks to her. Sometimes they touch her in offensive ways. Her whole workday is filled with this kind of behavior. Loretta has witnesses who say the same sort of thing happens to them in this office. They say that when they appealed to the boss to correct the situation, he just shrugged it off.

Do these situations constitute sexual harassment? What questions would you ask before deciding?

## An Easier Way

Court trials are long and costly. They also take a heavy emotional toll on all the people involved. Is there a simpler way to solve the problem of sexual harassment?

The ideal way to solve the problem of sexual harassment is to make sure it doesn't happen. Today, many employers run training sessions for new employees to discuss harassment and explain the company's rules. Some companies have regular, on-going talk sessions where men and women employees can speak frankly about offensive situations in the workplace.

Everyone learns in these talk sessions. For example, women find out that men are sometimes sexually harassed, too. It's possible for a female supervisor to make *quid pro quo* statements or suggestive remarks to the men who work for her. Or, a man might be really surprised when he learns that a female co-worker is uncomfortable with his comments on her figure. What he thinks is a compliment, she may think is a come-on. In talk sessions, co-workers learn to be honest and up-front right away with one another about offensive situations. Companies like the results: businesses run more smoothly when male and female employees treat each other with respect.

# Comprehension

## Think About it

1. What is *quid pro quo*?
2. What is a hostile work environment?
3. What is the first step in trying to stop sexual harassment?
4. How does an employee collect evidence for the court about sexual harassment?

## Write About It

Reread the four stories on pages 89 and 90. Has your opinion changed about the four situations? Do any of them describe a situation of sexual harassment? Explain.

**Instructor's Notes:** Have students read and answer the questions. **Write About It** can be used as a writing or discussion assignment.

# Comprehension: Recalling Facts/Character Traits

**A. Choose the best answer to each question. Fill in the circle.**

1. Who decides if a hostile environment exists?

   ○ **a.** the employer
   ○ **b.** co-workers
   ○ **c.** the courts

2. What is the main purpose of employee talk sessions?

   ○ **a.** to punish harassers
   ○ **b.** to discuss workplace problems
   ○ **c.** to learn company rules

**B. Read the paragraphs. Fill in the circle beside the most accurate character trait.**

For the third time that week, Don asked the new employee, Rita, out for a date. For the third time, Rita turned him down. "Listen," she said. "I already told you that I have a boyfriend and I don't want another one."

"I don't care how many boyfriends you have," said Don. "I really like you, and I'm going to keep asking 'til you say yes."

"I'd really hate to have to tell the boss about you," said Rita. "But if I have to, I will."

1. Rita is

   ○ **a.** honest.
   ○ **b.** bossy.
   ○ **c.** flirtatious.

2. Don is

   ○ **a.** sensitive.
   ○ **b.** angry.
   ○ **c.** insistent.

**Instructor's Notes:** Read the instructions with students. After students complete the exercises, review the answers.

# Comprehension: Writer's Tone and Purpose

When someone speaks, you hear the tone of voice. The tone gives you a clue to the speaker's attitude. For example, when someone says, "Oh, leave me alone!," the tone of voice tells you if the speaker is angry or amused.

Writers use a **tone**, too. When you read, you must figure out the tone from the way the writer uses words. Writers also have a **purpose**, or reason, for writing about a subject. The purpose may be to tell a story, to explain or describe something, or to persuade people to act or think in a certain way.

**How To Recognize a Writer's Tone and Purpose:**
1. Read the story or article carefully.
2. Look for loaded words like *ridiculous, stupid, perfect,* and phrases like *I think that*. These are clues that the writer is expressing an opinion.
3. Look for ideas that are presented step by step. The usual purpose of this kind of writing is to explain something.

**A. Read the paragraph.**

It's my guess that sexual harassment never happens in my office. If it did, it seems to me that the victim would complain about it right away.

**B. Answer the question. Fill in the circle.**

What is the writer's purpose?

- ○ 1. To tell a story about sexual harassment.
- ○ 2. To explain what sexual harassment is.
- ○ 3. To give an opinion about a particular office.

**Answer:** Choice 3. The clues are the words *It's my guess* and *It seems to me*. The paragraph does not tell a story or explain anything, so Choices 1 and 2 are incorrect.

**Instructor's Notes:** Discuss the tips with students. Have students complete the exercise. Discuss the answer and explanation with students. Have students write a paragraph in their journals and label it with the tone and purpose.

# Comprehension: Writer's Tone and Purpose

**Read the two paragraphs. Fill in the circle by the best answer for each sentence.**

A.  My friend Myra got tired of looking at all the girlie calendars around the office. She told our boss she thought they were offensive. The boss said, "Hey, these calendars were given to us by one of our important clients." So Myra took the girlie calendars down and put up calendars with baby pictures on them. She told the boss: "Another important client gave us these calendars."

1. The writer's main purpose is to

   ○ **a.** explain something.
   ○ **b.** tell a story.
   ○ **c.** express an opinion.

2. The writer's tone is

   ○ **a.** angry.
   ○ **b.** humorous.
   ○ **c.** sad.

B.  The way I see it, sexual harassment is a very confusing issue. What offends one person may not offend another person at all. From my point of view, some people are just too sensitive, and others are too tough to care. This problem will never get solved.

1. The writer's main purpose is to

   ○ **a.** express an opinion.
   ○ **b.** explain something.
   ○ **c.** tell a story.

2. Loaded words in the paragraph are

   ○ **a.** "may not offend."
   ○ **b.** "this problem."
   ○ **c.** "too sensitive."

**Instructor's Notes:**  After students complete the exercises, discuss their answers and have them tell why the other choices are incorrect.

# Language: Pronouns

You recall that a noun is a word that names a person, place or thing. A **pronoun** is a word that takes the place of a noun. The words in color are pronouns.

I me you he we him us they she it her them

Use a pronoun when you don't want to repeat the same noun over and over again. Notice the difference in these sentences:
1. Those workers aren't mean, but those workers are unaware of the problem.
2. Those workers aren't mean, but they are unaware of the problem.

When you read a pronoun in a sentence, check to be sure you know what noun that pronoun replaces.

**A. Read the sentences below. Circle each pronoun. Ask yourself: Who or what did something? Write the name that the circled pronoun stands for.**

1. Ruth Ann's sister talked to her. _____

2. She told Ruth Ann not to be worried. _____

3. Gary said, "You will not lose this job, Ruth Ann."

   _____

4. "The job is important to me," said Ruth Ann. _____

5. Gary talked about the company's employees and said,

   "We will learn to get along." _____

**B. Write a pronoun to use in place of the underlined words below.**

1. Rita and Don had a difference of opinion. _____

2. It seemed to Rita that Don was a pain. _____

3. Don was trying to be romantic. _____

**Instructor's Notes:** Review the definitions of nouns and pronouns with students. Have them complete the exercises. Check for incorrect use of subject and object pronouns.

# Life Skill: Being a Good Listener

Being a good listener is a useful skill. Sexual harassment can often be avoided if people discuss their different points of view. But such discussions only work if those involved are good listeners. It's very important to really hear and understand what others are saying. Here are some tips to help you improve your listening skills:

- Show that you are interested by looking at the speaker.
- Listen for the speaker's tone. It is often a clue to how someone is feeling.
- Observe the speaker's body language. Here, too, you can learn more about the speaker's message and feelings.
- Don't interrupt. Let the speaker finish before you state your case.
- When you respond to a speaker, begin your answer by repeating key ideas that he or she has mentioned. For example: "If I understand you correctly, you are saying that the women in this office feel a lack of respect." Such a response shows that you have really listened and gotten the message.
- Be willing to consider points of view that differ from yours.

Read what these two people are saying. Then explain which person has done a better job of listening and why.

### Dialog 1
*Speaker A:* No one calls the men in this office "honey." The men are called by their names and I want to be, too.
*Speaker B:* Look, doll, it's just a form of expression.

### Dialog 2
*Speaker A:* No one calls the men in this office "honey." The men are called by their names and I want to be, too.

*Speaker B:* Oh, you prefer to be called Rita? Is that what you mean? OK, Rita.

**Instructor's Notes:** Review the listening tips with students. Encourage them to think of other situations in which good listening skills could make a difference. Have them role-play these situations. Have students choose partners and read the dialogs aloud. This exercise may be used as a discussion or writing assignment. Use the Unit Review on page 125 to conclude the unit. Then assign *Reading for Today Workbook Six*, Unit 6.

# A Superstar Retires

## DISCUSSION

### Remember

Look at the picture. What do you think is happening? Have you ever watched a major league baseball game?

### Predict

Look at the picture and the story title. What do you think this story is about?

**Instructor's Notes:** Read the discussion questions with students. Discuss the story title and photo. Ask students if they recognize the man in the picture.

Retirement! The word brings many things to mind. You may think of an older person sitting in a rocking chair, always talking about the good old days. You may think of someone who depends on other people for support and cheer.

To *retire* means to stop one's usual career and rest. When a superstar retires, he or she is likely to feel that life is now less full. But one superstar didn't look at retirement that way.

Jackie Robinson was the first African American to play baseball in the major leagues. His life served an important purpose: to establish the right of other African Americans to play in the major leagues. When he retired, he didn't want to rest. He wanted to help African Americans in any way he could. He also had other interests.

Here is a list of some roles Jackie Robinson played after he retired from baseball.
- founder of a bank for African Americans
- founder of a low-income housing project
- public speaker for political candidates
- activist in the civil rights movement
- coach at the Harlem, New York, YMCA
- author of books and newspaper columns
- husband and father of three children

## Robinson's Admirers Speak

When Jackie Robinson began his baseball career in 1947, many people resented him. They didn't want an African American to play major-league baseball. But his accomplishments on and off the baseball field soon made many people admire him. Here's what some people have said about Jackie Robinson.

A fan from New York said, "He was our hero. We'd get on the subway, come rain or shine, and go out to Ebbets Field in Brooklyn to cheer for him. He was the perfect athlete. We all wanted to be just like him."

**Instructor's Notes:** Tell students that this article is nonfiction, a biography of Jackie Robinson. Explain that a biography is the story of someone's life. Have students read the next two pages silently. Have them underline words they don't recognize. Review the underlined words.

While Jackie was playing for the Dodgers, sports reporter Grantland Rice said, "He's the best man . . . that baseball knows today."

Leo Durocher, manager of the Brooklyn Dodgers when Jackie joined the team, said, "He was a great competitor who could do it all. He was a manager's dream. He was under a lot of pressure when he came up [to the major leagues], but he took it as gracefully as anyone. If I had to go to war, I'd want him on my side."

Dixie Walker, a teammate of Jackie's, said, "Me being a Southern boy . . . it wasn't easy for me to accept Jackie when he came up. At that time I was resentful of Jackie, and I make no bones about it. But he and I were shaking hands at the end."

Bowie Kuhn, former Baseball Commissioner, said, "No one surpassed his contribution to sports. His entire life was courage."

Perhaps most important is the way young African-American athletes remember Jackie Robinson. Althea Gibson became a superstar in tennis, but only after suffering some insults from Whites on tennis courts. She said, "I didn't know Jackie, but I followed him, as all Blacks did. And he helped smooth the way for the rest of us because he played by the rules and was such a gentleman. He walked with his head high and gave the rest of us respect. He opened doors."

# Vocabulary: Definitions

**Read each paragraph below. Notice how the other words in each sentence help define the new word. Match the vocabulary words with their meanings. Write the letter.**

achievements
discrimination
minorities
racial
segregated

When Jackie Robinson was growing up, African Americans and other **minorities** lived in a **segregated** society. Because of this **discrimination**, African Americans had not been allowed to play in national team sports. Many people did not want him to play in the major leagues. One of his greatest **achievements** was keeping his temper in the face of insults and **racial** slurs.

_____ 1. minorities

_____ 2. segregated

_____ 3. discrimination

_____ 4. achievements

_____ 5. racial

a. kept away from others

b. concerning races of people

c. deeds accomplished

d. unfair treatment

e. groups of people who are different in some way from most people

executive
generation
integrated
opponents
prejudice

Robinson opened the door for the next **generation** of African-American athletes. By the time he retired from baseball, most of his **opponents** had changed their minds about him and other teams were **integrated**, too. People felt less **prejudice** against African-American players, but there was still not a single African-American **executive** in baseball.

_____ 6. generation

_____ 7. opponents

_____ 8. integrated

_____ 9. prejudice

_____ 10. executive

f. unfair opinion

g. people born around the same time

h. manager of a business

i. opened to all races

j. rivals; competitors

**Instructor's Notes:** Read aloud the instructions and the words in color. Have students read the paragraphs and complete the exercises. Then discuss the clues that helped them match the words and definitions.

# Vocabulary: Prefixes

A **prefix** is a word part added to the beginning of a root word to change the word's meaning. Four of the prefixes we use most often mean *not, opposite of*, or *lack of*. Read the list below.

| Prefix | Example | Meaning |
|--------|---------|---------|
| un–  | unconscious | not conscious |
| in–  | incredible | not credible, not to be believed |
| im–  | immoral | not moral, not good |
| non– | nonverbal | not using words |

**Read each sentence and study the underlined word. Write the meaning of the word. Then write your own sentence using the word.**

1. Some people were inflexible in their desire to keep African Americans out of major-league baseball.

   _____

   _____

2. Jackie Robinson hated racial injustice and decided to help change it.

   _____

   _____

3. Robinson remained nonviolent in spite of receiving racial insults.

   _____

   _____

4. When he retired, Robinson was impatient to see other African Americans succeed in their careers.

   _____

   _____

**Instructor's Notes:** Read the definition of a *prefix* and the examples with students. Have students complete the exercise. Then review the sentences they wrote.

# Word Study: Accent Marks

In a word that has two or more syllables, one of the syllables is stressed. That syllable is said with more force than the others. An **accent mark** (´) placed after a syllable shows which syllable receives the stress. Look at the words in color and notice which syllable receives the stress. Then say the words aloud, stressing the correct syllable.

ē´ vən        up set´        ə fend´        rong´ fəl

Some words are pronounced in more than one way, depending on their meaning. The accent mark may shift to a different syllable. Look at the words in color and notice that each word has two different pronunciations. Say each word aloud, listening for the change in the accented syllable.

kən tent´   kän´ tent                ri bel´   reb´ əl

**A.  Read each word and its respelling. Write an accent mark after the syllable that is stressed. Check your work in a dictionary.**

   1. believe      bi lēv               2. athlete     ath lēt

   3. baseball     bās bȯl              4. career      kə rir

   5. founder      faun dər             6. major       mā jər

   7. purpose      pûr pəs              8. pressure    presh ər

   9. respect      ri spekt             10. resent      ri zent

  11. retire       ri tīr                12. surpass     sər pas

**B.  Read each sentence and circle the respelling of the word that makes sense in the sentence. Use the accent marks to help you.**

   1. Jackie Robinson had a fine (ri kȯrd´  rek´ ərd) as a baseball player.

   2. Robinson had to put up with some (in sults´  in´ səlts) because of his race.

   3. He was the (pûr´ fikt  pər fekt´) athlete.

**Instructor's Notes:** Discuss the information on accent marks with students. Have students complete the exercises. For A, have dictionaries available for students to check their answers. Provide help as needed. For B, have students read the sentences aloud with their answer choices.

## BACK TO THE STORY

■ ■ ■ ■ ■ ■ ■ ■ **Remember:** What have you learned about Jackie Robinson so far?

■ ■ ■ ■ ■ ■ ■ ■ ■ **Predict:** What do you expect to find out about Jackie Robinson in the rest of the story?

# A Superstar Retires

Since baseball began, great African-American ballplayers had been part of the sport. But they had played in segregated leagues. Executives in the major leagues had reflected the prejudice of many white fans by saying that African Americans weren't able to play in the major leagues. Actually, the executives and fans were simply not ready to accept African-American players.

Branch Rickey, owner of the Brooklyn Dodgers, was different from the other executives. By 1945 Rickey had already been in baseball for forty years. Ever since his days as a college baseball coach, Rickey had wanted to one day integrate the great American pastime.

Rickey knew that integration wasn't going to happen just by the passing of time. Some African-American player would have to be the first. In 1945 Rickey chose Jackie Robinson to be the first one.

### That "Special Something"

What drew Rickey's eye to Robinson? It wasn't just Robinson's achievements as a four-star athlete in school. It wasn't just that he was a superstar on an African-American baseball team. Rickey's scouts had traveled all over the country looking for the African-American player who had the "special something" that Rickey was looking for. He wanted someone with incredible athletic skill as well as extraordinary strength of character. The first African American in major-league ball would have to play like a champion. He would have to listen to jeers, racial slurs, and even threats from fans and players. He would also need to have a pure personal background that no one could attack.

Red Barber, a famous sports writer, said about Robinson, "He was educated and intelligent. He didn't drink or smoke. He had character. Rickey was absolutely certain that the first Black major-league player would have to be so strong that he could survive."

**Instructor's Notes:** Read the questions with students. Help students review and predict. Encourage them to share anything they know about Jackie Robinson or other minority sports figures.

## The Robinson-Rickey Meeting

When Rickey decided to consider hiring Jackie Robinson for the Dodgers, he called Robinson into his office. That meeting is now part of American history. Rickey explained that Robinson would be part of a great experiment—an experiment that would end segregated teams forever. If Robinson responded to his opponents by shouting and fighting back, the experiment would fail.

Robinson asked, "Do you mean you want a ballplayer who's afraid to fight back?"

Rickey answered, "I want a ballplayer with the guts *not* to fight back!"

The tools of this great experiment had to be expert ballplaying and the behavior of a saint. Robinson would have to remain calm in spite of any insults that opponents threw at him from the dugouts and stands.

*Jackie Robinson and Branch Rickey signed a historic contract in New York.*

The two men made a bargain. Rickey agreed to hire Robinson, and Robinson agreed to put up with the racial slurs for three years. After that time he could fight back with his own fiery temper. To begin the experiment, Robinson signed on with the Dodgers' minor-league team, the Montreal Royals. Then in April of 1947, Jackie Robinson played for the Dodgers at Ebbets Field in Brooklyn, New York. That day was the first time an African-American player had ever set foot on the field of a major-league baseball game.

## The First Years

Before Robinson's first Dodgers season began, some of his teammates signed a petition. It said that they didn't want to have an African American on their team. Branch Rickey told them to try it or quit. The players stayed, but they were unfriendly to Robinson in the clubhouse.

To rattle Robinson, some opposing players called him unpleasant names. Some drove the hard spikes of their baseball shoes into Robinson's legs as they slid into base. Many baseball fans hollered insults.

Through it all, Robinson kept his temper. He played like a skillful athlete, bringing victory after victory to the Dodgers. In the long run, his teammates rallied around him. Even the ones who had been prejudiced against him at first finally changed. His great performances and silent courage won him popularity.

The Robinson-Rickey experiment was clearly a total success. Jackie Robinson proved his worth to his team. Sports writers chose him "Rookie of the Year" in 1947 and "Most Valuable Player" in 1949. Later he was elected to the national Baseball Hall of Fame.

Even more important than Robinson's skill as a baseball player, was his personal example of courage and dignity. Robinson's life offers proof that people should be judged by their achievements and character rather than by their skin color. Many former opponents of integration saw for the first time that discrimination against minorities is unreasonable and immoral.

## Later Years

Jackie Robinson played for ten years in the major leagues. When he retired from baseball, he was not invited to move into an executive position with the Dodgers. Branch Rickey probably would have wanted him to do that, but Rickey was no longer around. Instead, the new management of the Dodgers hurt Robinson by trading him to the New York Giants. Since he didn't want to play for his old rivals, Robinson retired from baseball in 1957.

By this time, Robinson suffered from diabetes, a serious disease. It made him nearly blind. But he didn't let the disease slow him down. He put his energy and executive ability into a series of jobs and public projects. (*See the list again on page 105.*) He traveled, wrote, marched, and managed. He spoke out on political and social issues.

Robinson believed that African Americans would still have to struggle further against racial discrimination. He said, "I'm grateful for all the breaks, honors, and opportunities I've had. But I believe I won't have it made until the humblest Black kid in the most remote backwoods of America has it made."

On October 15, 1972, Jackie Robinson spoke to a World Series crowd in Cincinnati, Ohio. He recalled that he had come to baseball as a second baseman. He said that African-American athletes had not moved beyond second base. Maybe someday, he said, he would be able to look down the third-base line and see an African-American manager. Jackie Robinson died nine days later, at the age of fifty-three, after suffering a heart attack.

*Jackie Robinson and his wife left Washington, D.C. after he spoke about civil rights before the House of Representatives.*

### The Legacy

Since Robinson's death, two generations of African American athletes have greatly enriched American sports. At least 50 percent of the players on major-league football and baseball teams are African American. African Americans make up almost 80 percent of professional basketball players.

However, very few African Americans are in major-league coaching and executive positions today. One of the few is Hank (Henry) Aaron, a champion slugger who later became Director of Player Development for the Atlanta Braves. Aaron once said that his achievement would not have been possible without Robinson's example. He added, "I never dreamed of the big leagues until Robinson broke in with the Dodgers in 1947, when I was thirteen years old."

Much progress has occurred for African Americans and other minorities since Jackie Robinson signed on for Branch Rickey's "great experiment" over forty-five years ago. Would the integration of professional sports have happened eventually without him? Probably. Still, someone had to be the first. It's hard to imagine anyone taking on that huge task better than Jackie Robinson.

# Comprehension

### Think About It

1. Why was Jackie Robinson an important role model?
2. How did Robinson combat the prejudice and hostility of his teammates and the public?
3. What qualities was Branch Rickey looking for in the first African-American player in the major leagues?
4. Sum up the achievements of Jackie Robinson's life.

### Write About It

Suppose you could be the first person to achieve something important in a specific field. Describe what it would be. Include the qualities that would enable you to accomplish it.

**Instructor's Notes:** Have students read and answer the questions. **Write About It** can be used as a writing or discussion assignment.

# Comprehension: Recalling Facts/Writer's Tone and Purpose

**A. Answer each question using a complete sentence.**

1. Who was Branch Rickey?

   _____

   _____

2. Why did Branch Rickey choose Jackie Robinson to play on the Dodgers team?

   _____

   _____

3. When and where was the first integrated major-league baseball game played?

   _____

   _____

4. What did Robinson do when opponents yelled racial slurs at him?

   _____

   _____

**B. Think about the story you have just read. Underline the phrase below that tells the writer's purpose.**

1. to complain about racial prejudice

2. to compare Jackie Robinson and Branch Rickey

3. to describe the first African American to play major-league baseball

**C. Underline the word that identifies the writer's tone.**

angry        admiring        humorous

**Instructor's Notes:** After students complete the exercises, review the answers. For B and C, have students tell why they chose the answers they did and why the other choices are incorrect.

115

# Comprehension: Fact vs. Opinion

A **fact** is a bit of information that can be measured, observed, or proven. Facts answer questions about *who, what, where,* and *when.* An **opinion** is a statement of personal feeling or of a special view about something.

You'll find both facts and opinions in reading selections. Facts answer the readers' questions. Opinions express the feelings and views of the author and the characters. For example, read this sentence: *Baseball is the most exciting of all sports.* This is an opinion because we can't measure, observe, or prove how exciting baseball is compared with other sports.

**How To Recognize Facts and Opinions:**

1. Read the sentence or paragraph.
2. Decide whether it tells about something that can be measured, observed, or proved. If so, then it states a fact.
3. Does the sentence have clue words such as *I think, I feel, it seems,* or *it probably*? If so, it states an opinion.

NOTE: Not all opinions contain clue words such as those above.

**Read the paragraph below about Jackie Robinson. Then circle the word *fact* or *opinion* for each sentence.**

(1) Jackie Robinson was a great baseball player and a great man. (2) He was chosen baseball's Rookie of the Year and Most Valuable Player. (3) He founded a bank and a low-income housing project for African Americans. (4) Because of these achievements, Jackie Robinson is probably one of the greatest men of this century.

Sentence 1:   fact   opinion          Sentence 2:   fact   opinion

Sentence 3:   fact   opinion          Sentence 4:   fact   opinion

**Answers:** Sentences 1 and 4 are opinions because they cannot be measured, observed, or proven. Sentence 4 also has the clue word *probably.* Sentences 2 and 3 are facts. Written records prove these events happened.

**Instructor's Notes:** Discuss the tips with students. Read together the directions for the exercise and discuss the answer and explanations. Have students write fact and opinion sentences in their journals.

# Comprehension: Fact vs. Opinion

**A. Read the following paragraph. Then fill in the circle beside the correct answer to each question.**

Robinson was the youngest in a family of five children. His sister Wilma loved sports. His brother Edgar was a whiz on roller skates. Frank Robinson was excellent at track. Mack Robinson set a world record in sprinting and came in second to Jesse Owens at the 1936 Olympic Games. This athletic family probably inspired Jackie Robinson to do his best.

1. Most of the sentences in the paragraph state

    ○ **a.** facts.
    ○ **b.** opinions.
    ○ **c.** feelings.

2. In the paragraph, the clue to an opinion is the word

    ○ **a.** youngest.
    ○ **b.** probably.
    ○ **c.** inspired.

3. Mack Robinson's Olympic achievement is a matter of

    ○ **a.** opinion.
    ○ **b.** doubt.
    ○ **c.** fact.

**B. Refer to the story in this unit. Write a sentence that states a fact about Jackie Robinson. Then write a sentence giving your opinion about his years on the Dodgers team. In your opinion sentence, use clue words such as _I believe that..._ or _I think that...._**

1. Fact: _____

    _____

2. Opinion: _____

    _____

A **sentence** is a complete thought. Sometimes writers mistakenly run sentences together and create what is known as a **run-on**. The reader of a run-on can't tell where one thought ends and another begins.

> **Example:** Baseball is a national pastime in the United States Jackie Robinson was a national hero.
>
> These words are not a sentence. They are a run-on because two complete thoughts are run together. A reader could understand the thoughts more easily if they were separated into two sentences.
>
> **Example:** Baseball is a national pastime in the United States. Jackie Robinson was a national hero.

**A. Rewrite each of these run-ons to form two new sentences.**

1. The Dodgers used to be in Brooklyn now they are in Los Angeles.

_____

_____

2. Robinson was named Most Valuable Player in 1949 fans collected baseball cards with his picture.

_____

_____

**B. Rewrite the paragraph so that it has at least five complete sentences. Use a separate sheet of paper.**

Branch Rickey and Jackie Robinson made a bargain in the 1940s this historic agreement changed forever the game of baseball in the United States once people saw that superstars could be any race or any color, baseball was a far better sport. An important statement had been made in this country discrimination had no place on the playing field of any sport.

**Instructor's Notes:** Review the difference between a complete sentence and a run-on with students. Some students may need additional work on this skill.

# Life Skill: Reading Abbreviations

An **abbreviation** is a short form of a word or phrase. You've seen such abbreviations as *St.* for *Street* and *Ave.* for *Avenue*.

You will find special abbreviations on many forms and charts. Sometimes you won't know right away what an abbreviation stands for. However, you may be able to figure out the abbreviation from the context. Look at the chart below of facts about Jackie Robinson's baseball record.

| Jackie Robinson's Career Record | | | | | | | | | | |
|---|---|---|---|---|---|---|---|---|---|---|
| Year | Team | G. | AB. | R. | H. | 2B. | 3B. | H.R. | R.B.I. | Avg. |
| 1947 | Brooklyn | 151 | 590 | 125 | 175 | 31 | 5 | 12 | 48 | .297 |
| 1948 | Brooklyn | 147 | 574 | 108 | 170 | 38 | 8 | 12 | 85 | .296 |
| 1949 | Brooklyn | 156 | 593 | 122 | 203 | 38 | 12 | 16 | 124 | .342 |
| 1950 | Brooklyn | 144 | 518 | 99 | 170 | 39 | 4 | 14 | 81 | .328 |
| 1951 | Brooklyn | 153 | 548 | 106 | 185 | 33 | 7 | 19 | 88 | .338 |
| 1952 | Brooklyn | 149 | 510 | 104 | 157 | 17 | 3 | 19 | 75 | .308 |
| 1953 | Brooklyn | 136 | 484 | 109 | 159 | 34 | 7 | 12 | 95 | .329 |
| 1954 | Brooklyn | 124 | 386 | 62 | 120 | 22 | 4 | 15 | 59 | .311 |
| 1955 | Brooklyn | 105 | 317 | 51 | 81 | 6 | 2 | 8 | 36 | .256 |
| 1956 | Brooklyn | 117 | 357 | 61 | 98 | 15 | 2 | 10 | 43 | .275 |
| **Total** | | 1,382 | 4,877 | 947 | 1,518 | 273 | 54 | 137 | 734 | .311 |

**A. Study the abbreviations at the top of the chart. Then write the abbreviation that stands for each word or phrase below.**

1. games played _____       2. home runs       _____

3. at bat       _____       4. two-base hits       _____

5. hits       _____       6. runs batted in       _____

7. runs       _____       8. batting average _____

**B. Read across and down the chart to answer these questions.**

1. How many games did Robinson play in 1956? _____

2. In what two years did Robinson make 19 home runs? _____

   and _____

3. How many home runs did Robinson make in his whole

   career? _____

**Instructor's Notes:** Review the concept of abbreviations. Then discuss the contents of the career record chart. Have students complete the exercises. Use the Unit 7 Review on page 126 to conclude the unit. Then assign *Reading for Today Workbook Six*, Unit 7.

# Unit 1 Review

**A. Read the paragraph below. Write the missing vocabulary words to complete the sentences.**

| | | |
|---|---|---|
| recognition | influence | creative |
| audience | publish | reminisce |

You don't have to _____ a book to get _____

for your ideas and word pictures. When you _____ about your

childhood, write the memories down in a journal or diary. Your own family can be the

_____ for your stories. Your _____ writing

may have a great _____ on other people.

**B. Read the paragraph below. Fill in the circle beside the correct character trait.**

When Nelson visited his Aunt Liz, he always braced himself for a surprise. One
year she might be living in a trailer, the next year in a house by the sea. One year
her hair might be bright red, the next year a bunch of blonde curls. Nelson was
always eager to see what was in store for him when Aunt Liz opened the door.

1. Nelson is
   ○ a. curious
   ○ b. shy
   ○ c. lonely

2. Aunt Liz is
   ○ a. unhappy
   ○ b. unusual
   ○ c. frightened

**C. Write a short paragraph about a memory from your childhood. Use an adjective with each noun.**

_____

_____

_____

_____

_____

**A. Read the paragraph below. Write the missing vocabulary words to complete the sentences.**

| amendments | democracy | guarantee |
|---|---|---|
| Constitution | document | illegal |

The 13 states were more like different countries with their own laws before the

U.S. _____ was written in 1787. Leaders from the states met to

write a plan for a stronger government. The result was a _____

that began with the words "We, the people of the United States." It set up a form of

government called a _____ . Over the next 200 years, only 26

_____ have been added to the Constitution. These changes,

especially the Bill of Rights, helped to _____ all citizens certain

basic personal rights.

**B. Read each sentence carefully and find the cause. Fill in the circle beside your answer.**

1. The doctor treated the woman with leeches
   - ○ **a.** in his office on the main street.
   - ○ **b.** because she often had painful headaches.
   - ○ **c.** after closing the windows.

2. The dentist pulled a man's perfectly good front teeth
   - ○ **a.** and paid the man for them.
   - ○ **b.** which was a very painful process.
   - ○ **c.** because he needed them to make a set of false teeth for another patient.

3. The people in the State House were very hot as they wrote the Constitution
   - ○ **a.** because they closed the windows to keep out flies.
   - ○ **b.** which was signed on September 17, 1787.
   - ○ **c.** and kept all their plans a secret.

# Unit 3 Review

**A.** **Read the paragraph below. Write the missing vocabulary words to complete the sentences.**

| facial | reveals | behavior |
|--------|---------|----------|
| insight | observe | communication |

Body language is a form of _____ that is not limited to people.

Dogs, for example, use body and tail posture and _____

expressions to communicate with people and other dogs. A dog's _____

usually _____ its feelings. A relaxed dog with a wagging,

horizontal tail is smiling. However, a stiff-legged dog with an upright tail may be

ready to attack. Always _____ a strange dog's body language

before you approach the dog. Its behavior will give you an _____

into the dog's attitude toward you.

**B.** **Read each paragraph and the statements below it. Fill in the circle beside the best inference.**

1. As Nan walked down the street, a dog she didn't know came toward her. Nan stopped to greet the dog. The dog approached slowly, with its tail up and teeth showing. The dog was snarling.

   ○ **a.** The dog was greeting Nan warmly.
   ○ **b.** The dog wanted Nan to take it for a walk.
   ○ **c.** The dog was acting unfriendly and threatening.

2. Two dogs were in a yard together. Both were wagging their tails and moving toward each other in an easy-going manner. The large dog approached the small dog, standing on its hind legs and extending its front paws.

   ○ **a.** The dogs were getting ready to fight.
   ○ **b.** The large dog was asking the small dog to play.
   ○ **c.** The large dog was getting ready to go in the house to eat.

# Unit 4 Review

**A. Read the paragraph below. Write the missing vocabulary words to complete the sentences.**

| severe | sensitive | conceal |
|--------|-----------|---------|
| unbearable | overcome | physician |

After her stroke, Mary began to study karate at the suggestion of her

_____ . This type of exercise would help her _____

some of the physical problems caused by her stroke. Karate helps to stretch muscles,

but it is also a form of self-defense. In karate, one person delivers _____

blows to another person using the feet, elbows, hands, or knees. These blows are

often aimed at a _____ part of the body such as the stomach or

throat. Receiving such a blow can be _____ . Of course, in

Mary's class the students did not really hit each other. Still, at the beginning, Mary

had to _____ her nervousness. After she had been to a few

classes, she began to look forward to going.

**B. The events below are not in order. Write *1, 2, 3* and *4* to show the order in which events happened. Refer to the paragraph above to check the sequence.**

_____ Mary decided to take a karate class.

_____ Mary had a stroke.

_____ Mary began to look forward to karate class.

_____ Mary was nervous about karate.

**C. Write a short paragraph using the four sentences in part B. Use sequence words such as *before, after, while, during,* and *next* to put the events in sequence. Write your paragraph on a separate sheet of paper.**

# Unit 5 Review

**A. Read the paragraph below. Write the missing vocabulary words to complete the sentences.**

| apply | previous | qualify |
|---|---|---|
| accurate | financial | reference |

Carol wanted to buy a new VCR. She didn't have all the cash to pay for it, but she

could make a down payment. Before she went to the store, she examined her

_____ situation. Her car was now paid for. She had $300 in

savings and a good-paying job. Carol decided to _____ for credit

at the store. To _____ for a loan, she went to the store and filled

out a form. She listed her current and _____ employers and a

personal _____ . She knew that what she wrote must be

_____ .

**B. Read each question and write your conclusion.**

1. After reading the paragraph above, do you think Carol will qualify for a loan? Tell why you think this.

   _____

   _____

   _____

   _____

2. Suppose Carol had had trouble making her car payments on time. Do you think she will get credit to buy a VCR now? Tell why you think this.

   _____

   _____

   _____

## Unit 6 Review

**A. Read the paragraph below. Write the missing vocabulary words to complete the sentences.**

| harrassment | representative | offensive |
|---|---|---|
| conditions | supervisor | environment |

The _____ called the employees to a meeting. He wanted to

talk about the office _____ . Was _____

taking place? Were the working _____ comfortable for both

women and men? Was anything _____ happening day after day?

As a _____ of the employer, he wanted to make sure employees

had as few problems as possible.

**B. Read the paragraph. Fill in the circle beside the correct answer.**

A *hostile work environment* doesn't apply just to sexual harassment. The term is also used to tell about other problems in workplaces. For example, a work environment might be hostile to people with certain disabilities or to people who have language problems.

1. The writer's tone is

   ○ a. angry.
   ○ b. objective.
   ○ c. puzzled.

2. The writer's purpose is to

   ○ a. give a point of view.
   ○ b. tell a story.
   ○ c. explain a term.

**C. Write a short paragraph about someone you know. Use pronouns such as *I, he, she, it, him, her, we, us, they, them.***

_____

_____

_____

_____

# Unit 7 Review

**A. Read the paragraph below. Write the missing vocabulary words to complete the sentences.**

| integrated | racial | achievements |
| segregated | minorities | discrimination |

In the past, certain _____ , such as African Americans and

Hispanics, have faced _____ in jobs, schools, and housing. In

1954 the Supreme Court ruled that separate schools for African Americans and whites,

called _____ schools, were not legal. The Reverend Martin

Luther King, Jr., led the struggle against other types of _____

injustice. Important _____ have taken place in that struggle. For

example, public places such as bus stations and theaters are now _____ ,

but King's work remains unfinished.

**B. Write *fact* after each sentence below that states a fact. Write *opinion* after each sentence that gives an opinion. Circle any clue words that show a sentence is an opinion.**

I. Jackie Robinson was probably one of the greatest baseball players who ever lived.

_____

2. Robinson was elected to baseball's Hall of Fame in 1962. _____

3. I think Robinson must have had trouble keeping his temper when people shouted

insults at him. _____

4. After he retired, Robinson worked to help other African Americans achieve

success. _____

5. It appears that Robinson's achievements led to the success of other African

American athletes. _____

# Answer Key

## Unit 1

▶ **Page 11**

1. e
2. a
3. d
4. b
5. c
6. j
7. f
8. i
9. h
10. g

▶ **Page 12**

A. 1. d
2. b
3. c
4. a

B. 1. b
2. d
3. a
4. c

▶ **Page 13**

1. ap/peal     interest
2. view/point     way of looking at life
3. strug/gle     work hard
4. af/fect     move

▶ **Page 18**

Think About It
Discuss your answers with your instructor.

1. Cisneros grew up in the Mexican and U.S. culture, and most of her works are about the conflict between the culture of the family and that of the society and are based on memories from her childhood.

2. Answers might include mention of the following characters: a woman who returns home when her marriage doesn't work out; a Mexican dancer named Tristen who becomes famous in a San Antonio nightclub; children who buy Barbie doll clothes that smell like smoke and ashes; and children who go to Mexican movies.

3. Stories about people's memories of when they learned hard lessons about life are called coming-of-age stories.

4. Cisneros writes about experiences and feelings that everyone knows.

Write About It
Discuss your writing with your instructor.

▶ **Page 19**

1. b
2. c
3. a
4. a
5. b
6. c

▶ **Page 20**

B. 2, 3

▶ **Page 21**

A. 1, 4

B. 2, 3

▶ **Page 22**

A. 1. Cisneros has won <u>important</u> awards for her <u>original</u> work.

2. Poems by Cisneros can be <u>funny</u> and <u>sad</u>.

3. The <u>first</u> poems she wrote were published in 1980 as part of a <u>special</u> series.

4. Although it is a <u>major</u> form of communication, writing is an <u>independent</u> and <u>lonely</u> task.

**B.** 1–3. Discuss your answers with your instructor.

▶ **Page 23**

1. catalog
2. fiction
3. nonfiction
4. periodicals
5. librarian

# Unit 2
▶ **Page 27**

1. c
2. d
3. e
4. a
5. b
6. h
7. f
8. i
9. j
10. g

▶ **Page 28**

**B.** 1. a, (con)victs

2. b, re (fused)

3. b, ob (ject)
4. a, (con) tent
5. b, mi (nute)
6. a, (reb) els
7. b, re (belled)

▶ **Page 29**

**A.** 1. ba/sic     le/gal
2. a/mend     a/bove     a/ware
3. trav/el     clos/et     lem/on

**B.** 1. sec/ond
2. no/tice
3. mod/ern
4. im/age
5. o/bey
6. a/gain
7. a/larm
8. lim/it

▶ **Page 34**

Think About It

Discuss your answers with your instructor.

1. The Constitution sets up a democratic form of government and guarantees certain rights to the people.

2. The Constitution can be changed by amending it.

3. The Supreme Court interprets the Constitution in order to decide questions about people's rights.

4. The article described some of the rights the Constitution guarantees. It mentions becoming a citizen; providing an army, navy, and air force; providing mail service and one system of money for all the states; and guaranteeing freedom of religion and

a fair trial for someone charged with a crime. It described the daily life of the authors of the Constitution. It also mentioned some important cases decided by the Supreme Court.

Write About It

Discuss your writing with your instructor.

▶ **Page 35**

A. 1. b
   2. a

B. 1. b
   2. c
   3. a

▶ **Page 36**

A. 2

B. 1

▶ **Page 37**

A. 1. b
   2. a
   3. a

B. 1. b
   2. a
   3. c

▶ **Page 38**

1. The Declaration of Independence, written by Thomas Jefferson in 1776, declared that the American colonies were free of British rule.

2. If the Constitution were being written today, citizens of Philadelphia would read about it in *The Philadelphia Inquirer*.

3. Justice Sandra Day O'Connor is the first woman to serve on the United States Supreme Court.

▶ **Page 39**

Personal information on voter registration card will vary.

# Unit 3

▶ **Page 43**

1. b
2. c
3. a
4. e
5. d
6. g
7. f
8. i
9. j
10. h

▶ **Page 44**

A. 1. uncomfortable
   2. unsure
   3. unconscious
   4. unspoken

B. 1. nervousness
   2. friendliness
   3. tiredness
   4. consciousness

▶ **Page 45**

1–5. Sentences will vary.
1. pur/ple
2. sta/ble
3. tick/le
4. bub/ble
5. cack/le

▶ **Page 50**

<u>Think About It</u>

Discuss your answers with your instructor.

1. Half of what a person means is expressed in body language. Body language tells you more about what people are really thinking and feeling.

2. People that feel sure of themselves walk and stand tall and straight; they look you in the eye; they have a firm handshake; and they don't yell, point, or take up your space.

3. Nervous people slouch or shift their weight; they look down or around the room when speaking; they wiggle, blink, and lick their lips; and they have a cold, limp handshake.

4. Body language is a form of communication. Good body language can help you in social situations or in getting a job. Many nonverbal messages can give away your real feelings which might help or hurt you in certain situations. Other ways to "read" people include listening to their tone of voice, how fast they talk, and expressions they use. If body language and words don't match, people get mixed messages and are confused.

<u>Write About It</u>

Discuss your writing with your instructor.

▶ **Page 51**

A. 1. b
   2. c
   3. a
   4. b

B. b

C. a

▶ **Page 52**

A. Fact 1: Larry greeted Mr. Lorn with a firm handshake.
   Fact 2: As Larry introduced himself, he looked directly into Mr. Lorn's eyes.
   Fact 3: Both men were smiling when they sat down.

B. 1

▶ **Page 53**

A. 1. c
   2. b

B. 1. May taps her foot and sighs. She rubs her hand across her forehead. She talks very slowly when she answers Mrs. Rown's questions.
   2. May is uncomfortable about something —either the new job or talking to Mrs. Rown.

▶ **Page 54**

A. 1–6. Answers will vary.

B. 1–5. Answers will vary.

▶ **Page 55**

1–5. Answers will vary.

# Unit 4
▶ **Page 59**

1. c
2. e
3. d
4. b
5. a
6. i

7. f

8. j

9. h

10. g

▶ **Page 60**

A. 1. e

2. d

3. a

4. c

5. b

6. g

7. f

B. 1–6. Sentences will vary.

▶ **Page 61**

A. 1. 3

2. 3

B. 1. 2

2. 3

3. 1

C. Sentence will vary.

▶ **Page 66**

Think About It

Discuss your answers with your instructor.

1. The learning disability was dyslexia.

2. Mary came from a poor family. She had dropped out of school and had been in trouble with the law. She had two children and little money. She had had five heart attacks and a stroke which caused a memory loss and a long recovery. She was old for entering medical school, and she failed some of her early medical school courses.

3. She wrote to 15 medical schools and told them the story of her life. Finally one school gave her an interview. She impressed the dean and he gave her a chance.

4. Mary Groda overcame many difficulties in order to become a doctor. She became a doctor with a great talent for working with patients. (Answer may include some information from answer to #2.)

Write About It

Discuss your writing with your instructor.

▶ **Page 67**

A. 1. Two teachers in the Upward Bound program taught Mary to read.

2. Dyslexia is a learning disability that makes reading and writing difficult.

3. Mary graduated from college in 1980.

4. David read Mary's assignments to her.

5. Mary believed she could bring something special to the role of a physician.

6. Mary met David in karate class.

7. Mary remembers that picking strawberries was hard work.

B. b

▶ **Page 68**

3

▶ **Page 69**

A. 2, 4, 3, 1

B. 1. a

2. c

3. b

4. c

5. a

► **Page 70**

A. 1. b
   2. a
   3. a
   4. b

B. 1–4. Sentences will vary.

► **Page 71**

Personal information on medical form will vary.

# Unit 5

► **Page 75**

   1. c
   2. a
   3. e
   4. b
   5. d
   6. i
   7. h
   8. f
   9. j
   10. g

► **Page 76**

1. Carol talked to a counselor in the financial aid office.

2. She wanted to consider all the choices before becoming a borrower.

3. Carol's parents taught her to be a wise consumer.

4. She knows about buying on credit and understands her obligation to the creditor.

► **Page 77**

1. pay/a/ble, due

2. non/pay/ment, failure to pay
3. un/com/fort/a/ble, worried

► **Page 82**

Think About It

Discuss your answers with your instructor.

1. The advantage to buying on credit is you can buy things you need even though you don't have the money to pay for them right now. The disadvantage to buying on credit is you pay more.

2. You can write to the credit bureau and ask for a copy of your credit record.

3. You need a good credit rating; you should be aware of all charges and of your rights if you apply for credit; it's important to keep a good credit record; credit bureaus keep files on people; keep your credit payments to less than 15% of your income; you have rights as a consumer and can get a copy of your credit record; and you can get professional help if you get in trouble with debt.

Write About It

Discuss your writing with your instructor.

► **Page 83**

A. 1. A debt counselor can help with debt problems.

   2. Late payments and unpaid debts can ruin a credit record.

   3. Get your credit record at a credit bureau.

   4. Contact a debt counselor when you need help cleaning up a bad credit record.

   5. You pay more because finance charges increase the total cost.

6. Late payment information stays on your record 7 years after you settle the debt.

**B.** 1. cause
2. effect

▶ **Page 84**

**B.** Fact 1: Richard got a raise at his job.
Fact 2: He bought a new car and TV on credit.
Fact 3: He moved to a bigger house.
Fact 4: He is having trouble paying his monthly bills.

**C.** 3

▶ **Page 85**

**A.** 1. b
2. c
3. a

**B.** 1. Answers will vary.
2. They probably would not be able to get credit now.

▶ **Page 86**

**A.** 1. kept
2. fought
3. brought
4. stood

**B.** 1. saw
2. threw
3. given

▶ **Page 87**

Personal information on credit application will vary.

# Unit 6
▶ **Page 91**

1. c
2. e
3. d
4. b
5. a
6. i
7. j
8. g
9. h
10. f

▶ **Page 92**

1. **b.** ship
2. **a.** few
3. **c.** dreams
4. **c.** easy
5. **b.** desk
6. **a.** workers
7. **b.** cries

▶ **Page 93**

1. throw, cone
2. succeed, ago
3. truth, pool
4. patient, day
5. issue, book
6. spoil, boy
7. cloudy, loud
8. correct, ago
9. cooler, pool
10. legal, sweet

▶ **Page 98**

Think About It

Discuss your answers with your instructor.

1. *Quid pro quo* is a Latin term meaning "something in return for something."

2. A hostile work environment is a workplace where the employee suffers emotionally.

3. If sexual harassment happens, the first step is for the employee to file a complaint with her or his employer.

4. The employee needs to make careful notes about the time, place, and nature of each offensive event, a list of witnesses who heard or saw the event, and a list of witnesses who have experienced similar offenses.

Write About It

Discuss your writing with your instructor.

▶ **Page 99**

A. 1. c
   2. b

B. 1. a
   2. c

▶ **Page 100**

B. 3

▶ **Page 101**

A. 1. b
   2. b

B. 1. a
   2. c

▶ **Page 102**

A. 1. her, Ruth Ann
   2. She, Ruth Ann's sister
   3. You, Ruth Ann
   4. me, Ruth Ann
   5. We, the company's employees and Gary

B. 1. They

2. her
3. He

# Unit 7

▶ **Page 107**

1. e
2. a
3. d
4. c
5. b
6. g
7. j
8. i
9. f
10. h

▶ **Page 108**

1–4. Sentences will vary.
1. not flexible
2. lack of justice
3. not violent
4. not patient

▶ **Page 109**

A. 1. bi lēv´
   2. ath´ lēt
   3. bās´ bȯl
   4. kə rir´
   5. faủn´ dər
   6. mā´ jer
   7. pûr´ pəs
   8. presh´ ər
   9. ri spekt´
   10. ri zent´
   11. ri tīr´

12. sər pas´

**B.** 1. rek´ ərd
2. in´ sults
3. pûr´ fikt

▶ **Page 114**

Think About It

Discuss your answers with your instructor.

1. Robinson was the first African-American player in major league baseball, and he showed courage and dignity in all aspects of his life.

2. Robinson kept his temper in the face of insults and racial slurs. He played like a skillful athlete and brought victory to his team.

3. Rickey wanted someone with incredible athletic skill and extraordinary strength of character.

4. Robinson was the first African American to play baseball in the major leagues. He founded a bank for African Americans, he founded a low-income housing project, he was a public speaker and an activist in the civil rights movement, he was a coach, and he was the author of books and newspaper columns.

Write About It

Discuss your writing with your instructor.

▶ **Page 115**

**A.** 1. Branch Rickey was the owner of the Brooklyn Dodgers.
2. Rickey chose Robinson because of his athletic skill and strong character.
3. It was played in April of 1947 at Ebbets Field in Brooklyn, New York.
4. Robinson held his temper.

**B.** 3. to describe the first African American to play major-league baseball

**C.** admiring

▶ **Page 116**

Sentence 1: opinion
Sentence 2: fact
Sentence 3: fact
Sentence 4: opinion

▶ **Page 117**

**A.** 1. a
2. b
3. c

**B.** 1–2. Sentences will vary.

▶ **Page 118**

**A.** 1. The Dodgers used to be in Brooklyn. Now they are in Los Angeles.
2. Robinson was named Most Valuable Player in 1949. Fans collected baseball cards with his picture.

**B.** Branch Rickey and Jackie Robinson made a bargain in the 1940s. This historic agreement changed forever the game of baseball in the United States. Once people saw that superstars could be any race or any color, baseball was a far better sport. An important statement had been made in this country. Discrimination had no place on the playing field of any sport.

▶ **Page 119**

**A.** 1. G.
2. H.R.
3. A.B.
4. 2 B.
5. H.
6. R.B.I.

7. R.

8. Avg.

B. 1. 117

2. 1951, 1952

3. 137

# Unit 1 Review

▶ **Page 120**

A. publish
recognition
reminisce
audience
creative
influence

B. 1. a

2. b

C. Answers will vary. Discuss your paragraph with your instructor.

# Unit 2 Review

▶ **Page 121**

A. Constitution
document
democracy
amendments
guarantee

B. 1. b

2. c

3. a

# Unit 3 Review

▶ **Page 122**

A. communication
facial

behavior
reveals
observe
insight

B. 1. c

2. b

# Unit 4 Review

▶ **Page 123**

A. physician
overcome
severe
sensitive
unbearable
conceal

B. 2, 1, 4, 3

C. Answers will vary. Discuss your paragraph with your instructor.

# Unit 5 Review

▶ **Page 124**

A. financial
apply
qualify
previous
reference
accurate

B. 1. Yes. Carol will probably get credit because she has paid for her car, she has money in the bank, and she has a good-paying job.

2. She probably would not get credit now because of her credit history of late payments.

• • • • •  ————————————————————

# Unit 6 Review

▶ **Page 125**

A. supervisor
environment
harassment
conditions
offensive
representative

B. 1. b
2. c

C. Answers will vary. Discuss your
paragraph with your instructor.

---

# Unit 7 Review

▶ **Page 126**

A. minorities
discrimination
segregated
racial
achievements
integrated

B. 1. opinion, (probably)
2. fact
3. opinion, (I think)
4. fact
5. opinion, (It appears that)

# Word List

Below is a list of the 165 words that are presented to students in *Book Six* of *Reading for Today*. These words are introduced on vocabulary, word study, and life skill pages.

**A**

above
accent
accurate
accused
achievements
admiring
affect
alarm
amend
amendments
analogy
angry
appeal
apply
assist
athlete
audience
aware

**B**

basic
behavior
believe
border
borrower
bubble

**C**

castle
catalog
cheerful
childhood
commitment
communication
conceal
conditions
conflict
conscious
consciousness
constitute
Constitution
consumer
content
convict
convicted
counselor
create
creditor
culture
custom

**D**

dedication
defrost
democracy
disability

discrimination
document

**E**

emotions
environment
establish
executive

**F**

facial
fiction
financial
founder
friendliness

**G**

generation
gesture
guarantee

**H**

harassment
hostile
humorous

**I**

illegal
image

immoral
impatient
incredible
inflexible
influences
injustice
insight
installment
insults
integrated

**K**

kindness

**L**

legal
lemon
librarian
limit

**M**

major
minorities
minute
modern

**N**

nervousness
nonfiction

nonpayment
nonverbal
nonviolent
notify

**O**

obey
object
objective
obligation
observe
offensive
opponents
overcome

**P**

passion
pattern
payable
pencil
perfect
periodicals
physician
pickle
poems
posture
preheat
prejudice
pressure

previous
project
promotion
pronunciation
publish
purple

**Q**

qualifications
qualified

**R**

racial
react
rebel
record
refuse
register
relatives
representative
resent
respect
respelling
result
resume
retire
reveal

**S**

second
segregated
sensitive
sentence
severe
stable
struggle
supervisor
surpass

**T**

testify
thirteen
thoughtless
tickle
tiredness
tradition
trait
travel

**U**

unbearable
uncomfortable
unconscious
unfinished
unforgettable
unlace

unspoken
unsure

**V**

viewpoint

**W**

warrant

# Comprehension Terms

Below is a simple glossary of some reading comprehension terms covered in the *Reading for Today* program.

**cause:** the person, thing, or situation that produces a result; a cause tells why something happened

**character trait:** a way of behaving or acting that is typical of a specific person; what makes individuals unique and recognizable

**classify:** to put objects, facts, or ideas in groups with other things that they are like

**compare:** to say or show how two things are alike

**conclusion:** an opinion or judgment formed after putting facts together

**context:** all the words in a sentence or paragraph

**contrast:** to say or show how two things are different

**effect:** the outcome that results from a cause; an effect tells what happened

**fact:** a bit of information that can be measured, observed, or proven

**inference:** a judgment made by putting together new information with information already known

**judgment:** a value, decision, or opinion made about something based on some reasons

**main idea:** the overall point of a paragraph; may be stated or implied

**opinion:** a statement of personal feeling or a special view about something

**purpose:** the reason a writer has for writing, such as explaining something or persuading a reader to act or think in a certain way

**sequence:** the order in which things happen; time order

**tone:** the attitude a speaker or writer has about a subject

# Language Terms
● ● ● ● ●

Below is a simple glossary of some language terms covered in the *Reading for Today* program.

**abbreviation:** a short form of a word or group of words (*Dr.,* A.M., *St.*)

**adjective:** a word that describes a person, place, or thing by telling what kind, how many, or which (a *huge* tree)

**antonym:** a word with a meaning opposite to the meaning of another word (*bad, good*)

**apostrophe:** a mark of punctuation used to show that a word is possessive (*brother's*) or that it is a contraction (*it's*)

**comparison:** adding the endings *–er* and *–est* to some words to compare things (*older, oldest*)

**compound word:** a word made from two smaller words (*baseball*)

**contraction:** a shortened word or words made by leaving out or combining some letters (*can't, I'm*)

**fragment:** a group of words that is not a sentence because it is missing a subject or a predicate (*In the woods last week.*)

**irregular verb:** an action word that changes spelling instead of adding *–ed* to show past tense (*wrote, sang*)

**noun:** a word that names a person, place, or thing (*book, woman*)

**plural:** more than one (one brother, three *brothers*)

**possessive:** showing ownership (*brother's, brothers'*)

**predicate:** the part of a complete sentence that tells what is being done or felt (She *went to work early.*)

**prefix:** a word part added to the beginning of a word to change its meaning (*un*happy, *re*read)

**pronoun:** a word that takes the place of a noun (noun *man*, pronoun *he*)

**reflexive pronoun:** a pronoun made with *self* or *selves* (*herself, themselves*)

**run-on:** two complete thoughts, or sentences, run together (*He ate dinner late then he went to bed.*)

**subject:** the part of a complete sentence that tells who or what is doing or feeling something (*The busy people* hurried to finish their work.)

**suffix:** a word part added to the end of a word to change its meaning (happi*ness*, act*or*)

**tense:** the time of the action shown by a verb (present tense *wait*, past tense *waited*)

**verb:** a word that tells an action or a state of being (*ran, loved, is*)